A Guide to Prehistoric and Viking Shetland

A Guide to Prehistoric and Viking Shetland

by

Noel Fojut

Published by
The Shetland Times Ltd.,
Lerwick, Shetland.

Cover photograph:
Standing stone above Loch of Tingwall — the "Murder Stone".

A CIP catalogue record for this book is available from the British Library.

ISBN 0 900662 91 3

First edition 1981.
Second edition 1986.
Third edition 1994.

Printed and published by
The Shetland Times Ltd., Prince Alfred Street, Lerwick,
Shetland, ZE1 0EP, Scotland.

CONTENTS

PREFACE

THIS small book takes the interested amateur from the earliest traces of human habitation to the Norse settlement. It draws upon field evidence in the form of visible remains, and upon excavation results where these are available. Over five thousand years cannot be covered in detail in so small a space. The intention is rather to give a guide for visitors to Shetland (and hopefully Shetlanders) who want to know a little about archaeology, and an introduction to Shetland for those who know something about archaeology elsewhere.

The book falls into three sections: a description and discussion, roughly chronological, of Shetland's past as we understand it through archaeology; a gazetteer of the best and most representative of sites (enough to keep an energetic visitor busy for some weeks); and a series of area tours taking in a good number of these sites in reasonably short day trips.

This is not a definitive statement of how things were in the past. We have little evidence, and understand less of what we know. There are yawning gaps in our knowledge, whole centuries passing without any firmly dated information. Many generalisations are made here on the flimsiest of evidence, and it is the author's hope that readers will go out and look, think about what they see and go on to expand and deepen our understanding of society in those remote times. This is a skeleton of what archaeologists have established, but even fully fleshed the body of archaeological knowledge is a slender one.

In the dozen years since this book's first version appeared, we have lost two of the author's first guides, Tom Henderson and Peter Moar. Only Andrew Williamson remains of the Lerwick Museum triumvirate who first directed youthful enthusiasm for Shetland's archaeological potential into useful channels.

No-one can write an archaeological guide without a debt to those who have dug and surveyed before. The greatest debts are to those who have allowed unpublished information to be used and these include Peter Winham, Raymond Lamb, Gerry Bigelow, John Hedges, John Barber, John Hunter, Beverley Smith, Olwyn Owen, Niall Sharples and last, but not least, Shetland's own resident archaeologist, Val Turner. For help in the field and the office, and many heated discussions on windy sites, thanks are due to all those named above, and also Alasdair Whittle, Brian Smith, Pat and Neil Thomson, Anne Sinclair, Patrick Ashmore, Richard Hingley, Mike Brooks, Steve Dockrill, John Hunter, Tommy Watt and many more. Last, but certainly not least, thanks to the dozens of helpful, and often anonymous, Shetlanders who have pointed me, more or less accurately, into the peat hags in search of interesting heaps of stones, usually after much tea and hospitality.

This new version of an established guide is dedicated to Fiona Stewart, with thanks for support at every stage, and for the introduction to the delights of coastal defences.

Edinburgh 1993

THE PHYSICAL BACKGROUND

GEOGRAPHICAL accident and geological history have produced in Shetland an environment which is unique, on a large scale, in Britain, providing for Man a territory which, although habitable, is often barely so. On the edge of the coastal shelf, the island chain lies at the junction of North Sea and Atlantic Ocean, and the oceanic climate which banishes long winter frosts also keeps summer temperatures moderate. In a regime of adequate rainfall, with fairly equable temperatures, long summer days allow reasonable crops to be raised, while the short days of winter make for a dead season. The main obstacle to farming is the wind, both through its own effect as an agent of growth inhibition and as a carrier for a heavy load of fine particles of salt, picked up from the spray on the many coastal skerries and cliffs. Where this spray is most dense, along the exposed clifftops, nothing can grow but a mat of wiry grass and sea-pink, while even inland its effects are never absent, except where the force of the wind is broken by the drystone dykes so typical of rural Shetland.

Salt-spray and cliff vegetation on cliffs at Watsness

The land itself consists of the upper portion of a submerged chain of hills, parallel ridges of rock running north and south and accentuated by millions of years of erosion into a landscape of long, whale-backed hills, with narrow valleys. Deposition of clay, sand and gravel during the Ice Age has resulted in much of the land being poorly drained, and glacial erosion steepened some of the cliffs, but by and large Shetland retains its pre-glacial form. Land and water are inextricably entangled, for not only do long, drowned valleys reach deep into the land but the surface is scattered with thousands of small lochs, marshes and streams, so that an apparently short journey may become a major undertaking.

This, and the fact that the land is split up into fragments, numbering up to five hundred larger and smaller islands, of which only sixteen are now permanently

Ice-carved rock on Housay, Out Skerries.

inhabited, has led to the truism that the typical rural Shetlander is a "fisherman with a croft" as opposed to a "crofter with a boat" as used to be the case in nearby Orkney. Only in recent years has the sea ceased to be the main medium of transport: in 1793 a former resident of Nesting could say, "The roads, bridges, etc., are in the same state here as in every other part of Shetland; that is to say, there are none".

It has been the sea which, after bringing in the first and subsequent settlers, has allowed survival in years of poor harvest caused by late springs, wet summers and tempestuous autumns, which are all too frequent. Fish are, and were, abundant, both around the shores and in deeper waters, and such creatures as seals, whales, otters and seabirds have been exploited, often at great risk, from earliest days, while more static resources such as seabird eggs, seaweed and algae have always been welcome.

Behind the shoreline, which is slowly sinking relative to sea-level, lies the land. Mostly this is a bleak, rock-strewn landscape of heather and sedge, growing over deep peat, broken in places by signs of man's long perseverence in the form of the green patches of improved pasture. Tilled fields are generally small, poor and

Sand-filled inlets provide rich grazing: Burrafirth, Unst.

prone to waterlogging. Formerly, more land was cultivated, and traces of early agriculture are everywhere: indeed, as will be seen, the whole history of Shetland seems to show a decline in arable farming from early days onwards. Small bands of limestone have provided the most fertile soils, while localised areas of sand-accumulation behind beaches have allowed some extensive agriculture, although at the risk of catastrophic erosion, as around Quendale Bay. The higher ridges, hills and moors lie under a desolate blanket of peat, which has formed from centuries of accumulating vegetation debris. Trees are few, but the occasional clumps of scrub willow and birch on isolated holms and inaccessible cliffs, and the one solitary hazel bush, point to a greater former extent. Those cutting peat sometimes report finding quite substantial thicknesses of timber. This indicates that the present treeless landscape is not original, but the result of a combination of climatic change, grazing and soil deterioration. All the taller trees in the islands today have been planted and carefully protected: even in prehistoric times driftwood seems to have been used in great quantities, so trees may never have been very large or numerous.

The coastal lands merit a closer examination, for it has surely been here, where farms meet the fishing grounds, that much of Shetland life has been lived since the earliest days. Shetland, together with the west coast of the Outer Hebrides, is unusual in northern Britain in having a coastline which is slowly sinking, rather than rising. The weight of ice imposed on Scotland during the Ice Age depressed central areas while forcing up the periphery, including Shetland. Now that the ice has gone, the land is restoring its balance, so that central areas are rising while the edges sink. It is estimated that Shetland has been sinking at an average of slightly over one metre per thousand years for at least the last five thousand years. The effects on the coastline vary. On the outer coasts, rock-fringed cliffs were over-steepened by the ice, and in places are now being eroded, at the south end of Bressay for example. Many cliffs, however, are fairly stable, as witness the grassed-over rubble lying at the foot of such headlands as Herma Ness. Behind the rampart of the great cliffs lie two further types of shore. The first is a coast of low, rugged, rocky slopes, with low cliffs broken by small bays, typified by the shores of Sandness or Nesting. The second is the coast found around the long inlets, or voes, where storm waves lose their force to break on the gentle slopes which run down to, and under, the sea.

The slow sinking of the land, combined with ice erosion, has resulted in a plentiful supply of sand and shingle, which the waves have built up into an

Gentle slopes and drowned coastline of Weisdale Voe.

array of beaches, some of curious form, like the bayhead and baymouth bars of Dales Voe, or the tombolo which links St Ninian's Isle to the shore. Behind some of the larger beaches great spreads of sand have built up, as material blown from the foreshore has been trapped and stabilised by the roots of coarse grasses. These areas have provided fertile grazing, and where not too deep can be cultivated, but are always prone to erosion by the wind when their seaward faces are broken by over-grazing or careless removal of sand.

Areas around Jarlshof and Quendale, in the south, and Breakon, in Yell, have suffered repeatedly from blown sand, which can sterilise large areas of farmland and bury houses. But the attraction of these areas for settlers is shown by the constant renewal of half-buried villages at Jarlshof. Shetlanders early became hardened to occasional disaster in their bid to carve out a living.

Despite the first impression of rugged cliffs and barren moors, the true Shetland, that of the people, is that gentler coast around the sheltered voes, where long-worked fields run down to a small strip of shingle, and boats can be drawn above the waves. And it is on shores such as these that we find the first traces of man in Shetland - a settler embarking upon a five thousand year struggle against wind and wave, seeking a living among bare hills and in poor soils, at the end of the settled world.

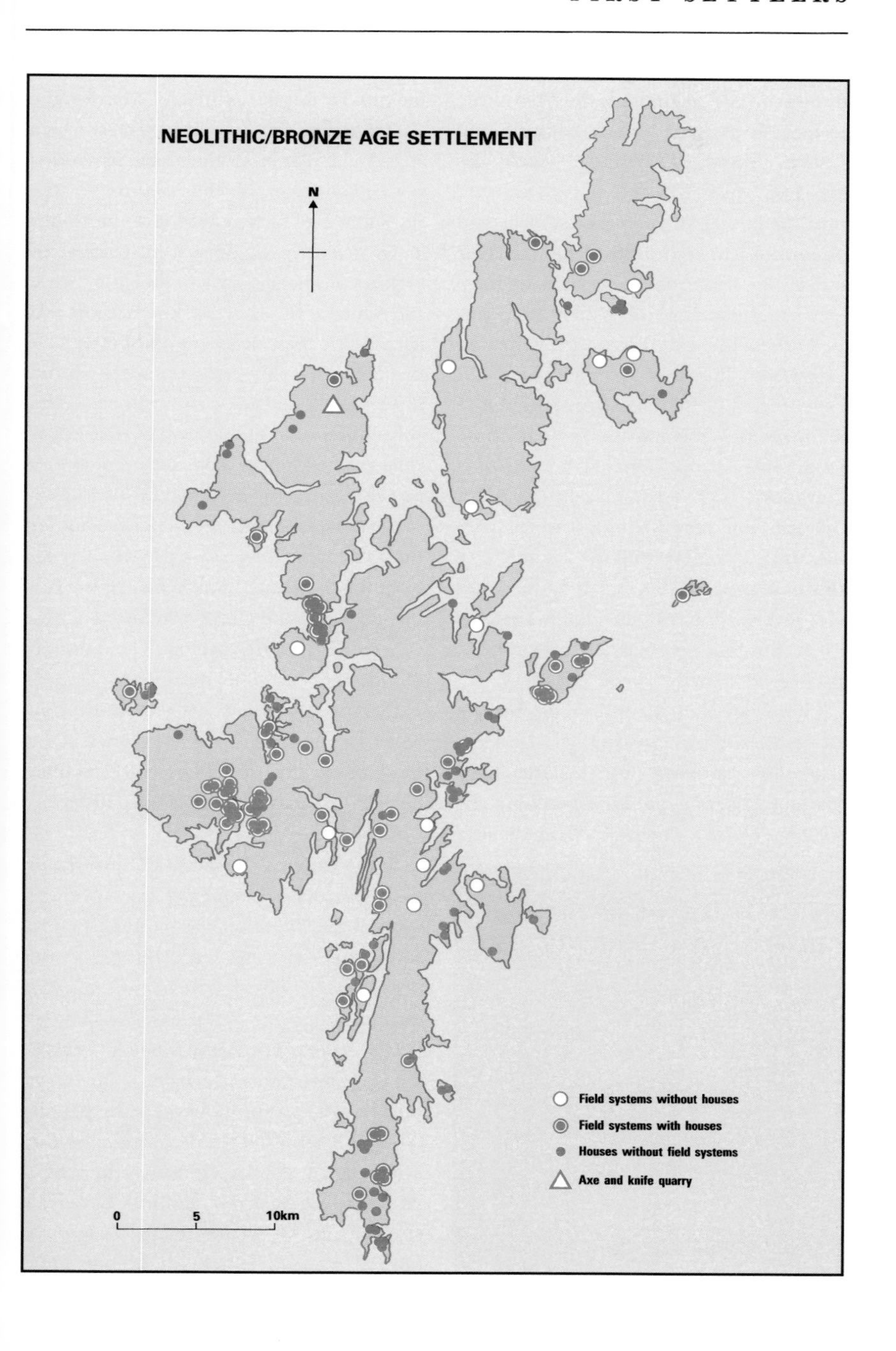
NEOLITHIC/BRONZE AGE SETTLEMENT
N
Field systems without houses
Field systems with houses
Houses without field systems
Axe and knife quarry
0
5
10km

ANYWHERE else in Scotland this account would begin with the Mesolithic period, during which small groups living a semi-nomadic life moved along the coastline and up the river valleys, hunting animals such as the red deer and exploiting the resources of forest, river and shore. Scotland is known to have been inhabited as early as 6500 BC, with the earliest identified settlement sites on the western islands of Rum and Jura. On the east coast, the characteristic blades of flint which formed the tools of these people have been found as far north as Caithness, with a single example from Orkney, but they are not known from Shetland. It may be that the islands were uninhabited at this period, or that Mesolithic hunters did reach this far north, but that no evidence has yet been discovered.

There can have been no real obstacle to enterprising groups of hunter-fishermen moving north, for they possessed boats capable of reaching the Western Isles. Perhaps Orkney and Shetland were explored and found largely lacking in the necessities of life, for the sparseness of the vegetation and the lack of large land animals may have precluded permanent use of the islands in the nomadic life cycle: there is some doubt as to whether red deer were present in Orkney naturally, or whether they were introduced by the earliest settlers. If Mesolithic man did settle in Shetland, it is likely that his encampments would have been beside the shore. The subsequent rise in sea-level of more than nine metres would have submerged any possible remains: little would be known of the coastal Mesolithic elsewhere but for the gradual falling of sea-level in most parts of Scotland, which has preserved the shell-mounds and artefact scatters characteristic of this period. The question of whether or not there was a pre-agrarian settlement of Shetland may never be resolved, but for the present we must accept that the earliest traces of man belong to a culture with a very different way of life.

One of Shetland's earliest settlements lay under this house at Scord of Brouster.

Some time before 3000 BC groups of early farmers, belonging to the stage termed the Neolithic, were established in Shetland around Sumburgh, and presumably elsewhere. One of the intriguing aspects of this early settlement is that we do not know when it began. The earliest dates are from a burial at Sumburgh, presumably made by people already established in the islands by the latter part of the fourth millennium BC. At Ward of Shurton, behind Lerwick, similar dates came from below a boundary wall, which might not be a likely first construction for settlers in a land with no natural predators. Similarly, at Scord of Brouster, the earliest dates came from the second of the houses built there, which lay above the traces of an earlier wooden house. However, such is the nature of archaeology that it would be surprising if we did find the earliest evidence in our rather haphazard investigations, and even if we did, it would be impossible to prove that we had found the first settlement without excavating and dating every site: and even then the first site of all might have been destroyed long ago.

It is surely significant that, by the time we do have evidence, the culture of the Shetlanders, as represented by manmade objects, had already developed distinct differences from that of their southern neighbours. The earliest pottery has a style clearly related to that found at Orcadian settlements of a slightly later date (Rinyo, Skara Brae, Noltland and Barnhouse), but is nevertheless different enough to be readily distinguishable. Early houses, too, show common features with those of Orkney, but are quite clearly the product of a different area, being oval, rather than round or sub-rectangular, and built in a style which takes account of differences in materials. This all points to the fact that Shetland was settled sufficiently long before our earliest evidence for these peculiarities to have had time to develop as a response to local conditions and materials. For all we know, the very first houses may have sunk below the sea, or been quarried away by later builders, but we can guess that they would have been constructed a little before 3500 BC, and by either descendants or contemporaries of the earliest settlers of Orkney. It would not have taken these settlers long to develop the distinctive character and culture which have marked Shetlanders ever since.

Who were these early farmers? The weight of evidence indicates that they were descended from members of a general immigration into northern Britain around 4000 BC. The possible ancestors of the early Shetlanders, a mixture of early hunter - gatherers and immigrant farmers, were established on Deeside by the early years of the fourth millennium BC, and probably reached Orkney not much later. From there it was a short step to Shetland.

The first settlers arrived in family-sized groups, bringing with them the technology of farming. Grain was known, both barley and wheat (though barley alone has been traced in Shetland). Oats arrived later. The tools of early cultivation, ancestors to the spade and the plough, must have arrived at the same time as grain. Sheep and cattle arrived early, for their bones are present in early settlement sites, with cattle apparently in the majority. Implements for spinning and weaving wool, and dressing skins, would have arrived as well. The pig is probably a later introduction, and this animal, originally a woodland creature, never seems to have been quite as much at home in Shetland as it was elsewhere in the north. It cannot be doubted that other items arrived of which we have no evidence, such as green crops like goosefoot and sorrel. The dog would have come as companion and helper to the earliest herdsmen.

How was this varied load of imports carried ? The only British boats known from this period are clumsy dug-out canoes and plank-built craft, hard to handle even on placid inland waters and incapable of carrying any bulky or awkward load. However, there were probably much larger boats built, on the pattern of the Irish curragh, from skins over a wooden frame. Such vessels might also have served as roofing for the first shelters erected by the immigrants, a use of obsolete boats still practised in Shetland to the present day. Some fine recent examples can be seen around Ulsta and Brough, in Yell, although these modern roofs are formed by boats which are much more substantially built than those suggested for the Neolithic.

It may be that these people arrived in some strength, rather than gradually building up their numbers over centuries. The reason for this hypothesis is that where there is extensive visible evidence for early agriculture, as in the West Mainland, the land seems to have been divided by substantial walls which run across country for long distances, cutting the countryside into large units, which are then subdivided by lesser field boundaries. This apparently early concern with land division seems to

A modern example of an age-old practice: boat-roofed shed at Brough, Yell.

Large blocks indicate ruined houses, set in rough enclosures dotted with field clearance cairns at Pinhoulland, near Walls.

indicate that people were present, or expected, in sizeable numbers at an early date.

Many remote parts of upland Britain hold traces of early settlement in the form of walls, fields and, more rarely, houses, most particularly where subsequent growth and later removal of peat have helped to preserve remains. It seems likely that this vestigial evidence represents patterns of land use once common to most of Britain, but since lost in the areas under later farms. Shetland, together with Dartmoor at the opposite end of Britain, and western Ireland, provides some of the best of this early evidence. Surprisingly, the fact that there were numerous Neolithic or Bronze Age remains in Shetland, other than burial cairns, seems to have escaped notice until the late 1930s. Today we know that there are a larger number of Neolithic and Bronze Age houses visible on the surface in Shetland than in any other area of comparable size in Britain, possibly than anywhere else in northern Europe. Almost everything that is known about life in the Neolithic is the result of the work of a few dedicated investigators since the Second World War. Excavations have been few in number, and survey and field observation provides most of our knowledge. The key to our understanding are the survey and excavation work of Charles Calder at a number of sites (Gruting School (19),

Ness of Gruting (20), Stanydale (18), etc) in the 1940s and 50s and the excavations by Alasdair Whittle at Scord of Brouster (15) in the late 1970s.

The best area in which to see Neolithic remains is the West Mainland. From Loch of Grunnavoe north, via Bridge of Walls, Voxterby and Sulma Water to the sea, a distance of six miles, there is alway some item of this period in view, be it a burial cairn, a series of field walls or a ruined farmhouse. Small mounds of stones cleared from early fields lie everywhere, and often close inspection of these will produce early stone plough-shares, discarded after damage while ploughing. Nor is this the only part of Shetland, for in addition to remains throughout Walls and Sandness, extensive traces of early agriculture can be seen in Nesting, Aithsting, Delting and Northmavine (particularly around Mavis Grind), and also in the more remote parts of Yell and Whalsay. Even the smaller islands, such as Fair Isle, Out Skerries and Foula, were settled by the start of the Bronze Age.

A pre-Iron Age wall emerging from beneath old peat cuttings at Brunt Hamarsland, Gott.

Anywhere that peat is being cut is worth investigating (taking care not to damage peat banks). Even nowadays it is not uncommon for the observant visitor to discover new houses and field walls once away from the more accessible parts of the islands. That so much does survive is mainly due to the growth of peat from the later Neolithic onwards, which buried the ruins of early farms. It is no coincidence that it is in those parts of Shetland where recent peat cutting has been most extensive that these remains are most evident. Areas stripped earlier seem to have had most of their prehistoric remains removed for use as building stone. Good examples of houses recently emerged from the peat can be seen at Newing, alongside the coastal road from Skellister to North Nesting (12).

Although this archaeological landscape is complex, it can, for the sake of convenience, be broken down into elements: houses and other formerly roofed structures; clearance cairns; field dykes and major boundary dykes. In addition are many larger cairns, some with burial chambers, which are a product of other than economic activity. And finally, we must consider the hidden evidence, only revealed by excavation, of crops, livestock, tools and other artefacts.

About 160 houses have so far been identified in the style which goes by the clumsy name of Neolithic-Bronze Age, sometimes called, for brevity and in tribute to their first investigator, ''Calder'' houses. Their ungainly name is outdated, for we now know that such houses were in use well into the Iron Age. A typical house ruin is a low oval bank of rubble with a hollow centre. The central hollow may show traces of alcoves around each side, and a depression at one end, marking the entrance, may be visible. The inner ends of the entrance, and the projections between alcoves, may be formed by massive upright blocks ("orthostats"). Overall dimensions are in the order of ten metres by seven, but vary greatly. Often the foundations of houses occur in small groups, with associated field walls straggling off across the surrounding landscape.

Excavations at Ness of Gruting, Gruting School, Stanydale, Sumburgh, Scord of Brouster and Kebister have given us a good idea of the construction of these houses. Walls are thick, faced with heavy stones and cored with rubble and earth, a technique used until recently all over the Highlands and Islands. The interior had two distinct levels. A central area, lower than the rest, generally held a large hearth, upon which peat was burned. Small, stone-lined drains ran

This house at Trolligarts shows the simple oval plan which may be slightly earlier in date than the transepted form.

The Benie Hoose, Whalsay, shows the thick walls and subdivided interior chamber of the transepted form of prehistoric house.

More typical of prehistoric house sites is this small example in Homisdale, Fair Isle.

from this area out under the entrance. Alcoves around the inside of the house wall were set higher, sometimes with raised sills and usually with paved floors. These alcoves are generally interpreted as bed-recesses.

In the course of excavation and field observation, two general classes of oval house have been identified. One is as described above, while the other, which is less frequently noted, has an oval form lacking alcoves but provided instead with small oval cells in the thickness of the wall. Houses of both types often have a curving wall outside the entrance, a porch, which would be essential in windy Shetland. Because only foundations remain, reconstruction of the form of these houses is tentative, but the evidence of post-holes and parallels with later structures of similar type allow us to assume that they had low walls with a heather and sod roof, pitched at a low angle and arranged on the walltop in such a fashion that the water drained from the roof onto the wall head, which would have been sealed with clay. The houses would have been low and dark, and doubtless smoky. Most daily tasks would have taken place around the outside of the house, with the inhabitants perhaps sitting on the doorstep in rainy weather to chip out quartz implements or knead clay for pottery.

It is not known whether all of the small groups of two, three or four houses which are typical of prehistoric Shetland represent true villages or are the remains of a succession of houses, each built upon the disuse of the previous one. At Brouster the evidence suggested the latter. Settlements are normally sited near to fresh water, but generally stand some distance from the sea shore, being most characteristically behind the best land, as seen from the sea. This makes economic sense, as it is wasteful to build houses upon the best farmland. These houses are found in higher and more exposed locations than more recent settlement, and this may support the suggestion that the climate was rather better in the Neolithic, and deteriorated thereafter. It is also a strong possibility that there were originally settlements nearer the sea and that these, being on lower ground, have more generally been built over in later times. This still happens today, for only a few years ago an un-noticed prehistoric house not far north of Lerwick was quarried away by accident during house rebuilding, and only identified from pottery found some time later in the dumped rubble.

Around the houses, and sometimes spreading a considerable distance from them, are often found mounds of medium-sized stones. These are usually part-buried in the peat, showing no more than a small patch of stones, yet on excavation have proved to reach diameters of three metres and more, and heights of over one metre above the sub-peat ground level. These cairns represent the results of many generations of field clearance, and are characteristically sorted, with the larger stones towards the base. This represents the pattern of preparing land for ploughing, with large stones removed early in the process, and then smaller stones being progressively eliminated once the land was broken in to cultivation. It seems likely that poor land management may have contributed to a deteriorating climate in causing the gradual impoverishment of the soil. Where pre-agricultural soils have survived below cairns and the walls of houses, these are much deeper and richer than the thin, acid, soils which characterise most of the upper hillslopes today. Indeed, this deterioration may, in turn, have hastened the growth of peat on waterlogged soils, so that early man may have inadvertantly helped to create the conditions which have preserved the remains of his settlements up to the present day.

A major boundary dyke appears through thin peat near Clousta.

Running among the cairns are stretches of low walling, which appear to split the land up into small fields of irregular shape. These often link clearance cairns together, so as to leave the maximum plantable area clear. Excavation of stretches of wall at Brouster has shown that, while they may link pre-existing cairns, sometimes they are earlier, with cairns later accumulated along their length. Although their foundations vary greatly in thickness, most cannot have stood high enough to provide a stockproof wall of stone, especially against the Shetland sheep, which can clear considerable heights when frightened. Perhaps these walls served the dual function of dividing patches of land worked by different persons and of absorbing odd stones found during cultivation: they are partly land divisions and partly linear clearance cairns. It is also possible that they are the surviving portions of walls made of stones and turf, such as are still sometimes seen today, particularly in Unst. If this is the case, then such walls might have been higher than the present stony banks would suggest. This, like so many of Shetland's archaeological problems, requires more thorough investigation.

In a rather different category are the large dykes which run semi-continuously across country, sometimes for several miles. These may be very substantial and run almost straight, apparently aligned with hilltops or burial cairns. The stones used may be very large indeed, and because of their solid nature many of these walls have survived to be adopted as boundaries between scattalds (township grazing lands), although

Many early land divisions may have been mainly of turf: two turf dykes and their drystone successor on Fair Isle. These are probably Medieval, but reflect much older divisions.

whether this represents continuity of boundaries over thousands of years is questionable. Good examples of these massive dykes can be seen to the north of the Walls road just beyond Bridge of Walls, and south of the Sandness road just beyond Scord of Brouster. A particularly intriguing example runs from the settlement at Brouster north-east into a bog, reappears from the far side and then runs up the hill into the distance. Further evidence for the early date of these large dykes is that where they run past areas of small fields associated with oval house ruins they are frequently seen to predate the field dykes, which run up to the large dykes and stop, sometimes being continued on the far side after a displacement of some metres. The most impressive example of all is probably the Funzie Girt (1), on Fetlar, which divides the north-eastern part of that island.

The major dykes partition the landscape into irregular areas of about 100 to 200 hectares. These dykes may have served to split up the islands among early groups of settlers. Their location on shoulders and ridges certainly makes them look more like boundaries than field walls, though they often link the upper walls of land which may have been cleared early in the settlement process. They very clearly postdate some of the hilltop burial cairns. It looks as if the earliest settlers of Shetland realised, not long after their arrival, that sufficient people would be coming to make a division of the islands into territories not only desirable but essential. This implies that there was a substantial population, perhaps several thousands or as many as ten thousand persons, and that these people were using most of the land in an organised fashion. The Neolithic was not, as is sometimes assumed, a period of ignorance, but was in fact characterised by organised agriculture and, as will be seen, an organised religion and great skill in the manufacture of objects, both for utilitarian and ornamental purposes. Therefore a sophisticated approach to the division of land is not at all impossible.

The low mound of Isbister cairn is fronted by a crescentic facade, with a central passage leading to the burial chamber.

As noted already, the earliest date for human presence in Shetland comes from a burial place,and for many years the chambered cairns were all that had been recognised in the way of Neolithic stuctures. This concern for the dead of the community enables us to reconstruct something of the less tangible side of prehistory, the beliefs and observances of Neolithic man. Indirectly, burial practices give evidence about social structure and, where gifts are placed with the dead, material culture.

Two methods of burial are known

from Neolithic Shetland. That which has left the most noticeable remains is the practice of inhumation in stone-built chambers below large cairns of stones: the well-known chambered cairns. Less well-known is the practice of burial in stone boxes, or cists, made of large flat slabs, but not provided with any permanent surface marker. It was formerly thought that cists, in which pottery of Bronze Age type has been found on some occasions, were uniformly of later date than cairns, with a transition marked by the construction of small round cairns over cist burials. While a good number of cists do seem to belong to the Bronze Age, or even later times, excavations at Sumburgh have shown that collective burials were being made in massive cists from the beginning. In fact the first chambered cairns may be somewhat later in date, with the sequence running: large cists with multiple burials, chambered cairns, individual burials in cists below cairns, individual burials in cists. Cremation does not appear until well into the Bronze Age.

The many chambered cairns, which occupy prominent positions on tops or shoulders of hills, are often disappointing on closer examination. Of the long cairns such as are found in Orkney, only one

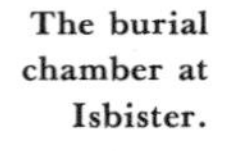

The burial chamber at Isbister.

example is known, and this is sadly reduced to a jumble of stones. A second example is suspected, but has not been investigated. The common form of chambered cairn in the islands is almost unique to Shetland, with a very few examples elsewhere in the north. This is the heel-shaped cairn, so called because of its plan, which resembles the heel of a shoe in being oval, with a concave facade cutting into one end. From the centre of this facade, which is more carefully built than the rest of the cairn, a narrow passage leads back into the burial chamber. This is commonly sub-rectangular, with one or more small alcoves opening out from the main area. The roof of the main chamber is generally formed by corbelling, while alcoves and entrance passages are lintelled.

One of the remarkable facts about these cairns is their range of size, from the massive piles of Punds Water (49), Vementry (53) and Daney's Loch to miniature versions such as that at Pettigarth's Field (40). Diameters vary from twenty to under four metres. The largest cairns seem to have been built in two stages, with the provision of a round cairn above the burial chamber followed by the construction of the elaborate facade. Unlike many cairns in more southerly parts, the facades seem to have been added at a time when the burial chambers were still open, and we may be looking at original planned shapes rather than the results of a series of modifications. Against this general pattern can be set the puzzling March Cairn (47), in Eshaness, where the chamber was entered by a passage from one of the sides that did not have a facade.

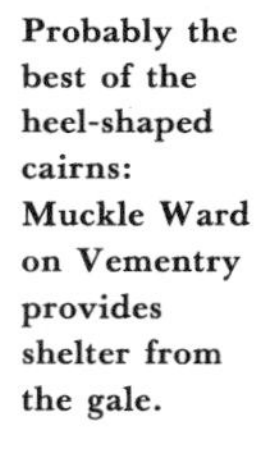

Probably the best of the heel-shaped cairns: Muckle Ward on Vementry provides shelter from the gale.

The concave facade of the Shetland cairns has been found to occur in a number of house sites also, notably at the site excavated in the 1970s during airport extensions at Sumburgh. It is possible that the cairns were copying a common house style, or vice versa. At Sumburgh the facade was added to an existing house, parallelling the elaboration of cairns mentioned above. Certainly the scanty fragments of pottery from cairns match closely those from excavated houses, thus supporting a similar date.

The miniature chamber of the robbed-out cairn at Pettigarths Field, Whalsay.

Both cists and cairns imply some measure of special treatment, for it seems unlikely there were ever enough of these burial places for everyone who died to be placed inside one. This is even more the case with cists sealed below cairns, where numbers were strictly limited, than it was with chambered cairns, which could be used so long as they were left open. The simple expedient of shovelling up the remains of earlier burials, to make way for the new occupant, is known from chambered tombs elsewhere. In some cases the bones seem to have been carefully bagged and stowed away in a side recess. It is generally believed that, even if tombs were cleared periodically, only a small proportion of the population can have been laid to rest in such style. Presumably most bodies were deposited, without burial chamber or memorial, into the ground, although they may have been cremated or disposed of at sea.

We have no way of knowing what factors led to the selection of certain individuals for burial in cairns. They may have been members of a ruling class or family, a priestly elect, or individuals linked by some more tenuous trait, perhaps a "propitious" time of birth or a particular combination of physical features. Work outside Shetland has shown that cairns may contain a wide range of ages and members of both sexes. As yet no convincing anatomical "family likenesses" have been recognised in the individuals buried in any one tomb. The only clear fact that emerges is that some tombs were in use for centuries. This must mean that few members of any one generation could have been interred in the chamber, supporting the idea of a quite exclusive elite. Unfortunately, little evidence is forthcoming from Shetland, for buried bone is not preserved well here, due to acid soil conditions, and most cairn excavations took place before techniques for finding fragmentary bone remains were well developed. Only one recent chambered cairn excavation has taken place, at Outnabreck above Scord Quarry at Scalloway, but here no evidence of the burials survived.

To continue the theme of a select class or group within Neolithic society, mention must be made of the so-called "temples" identified at Yoxie (Whalsay) (3) and Stanydale (West Mainland) (18). Called temples because of their similarity of plan with known ritual sites in Malta, they were excavated in the days when all innovations in British prehistory were held to have come from the Mediterranean region. About Yoxie nothing needs to be said, for excavation of more examples of early houses has shown that the plan of Yoxie is repeated in many other sites, and that the "forecourt" of the "temple" is nothing but a windbreak at the door of a very ordinary house.

Stanydale, however, is a wholly different case. Now partially restored, it is a house of normal plan, with the usual alcoves, and a very carefully built concave facade flanking the entrance, as at Sumburgh. The remarkable feature of Stanydale is its great size: it is about twice as large as any other excavated house, measuring no less than thirteen metres

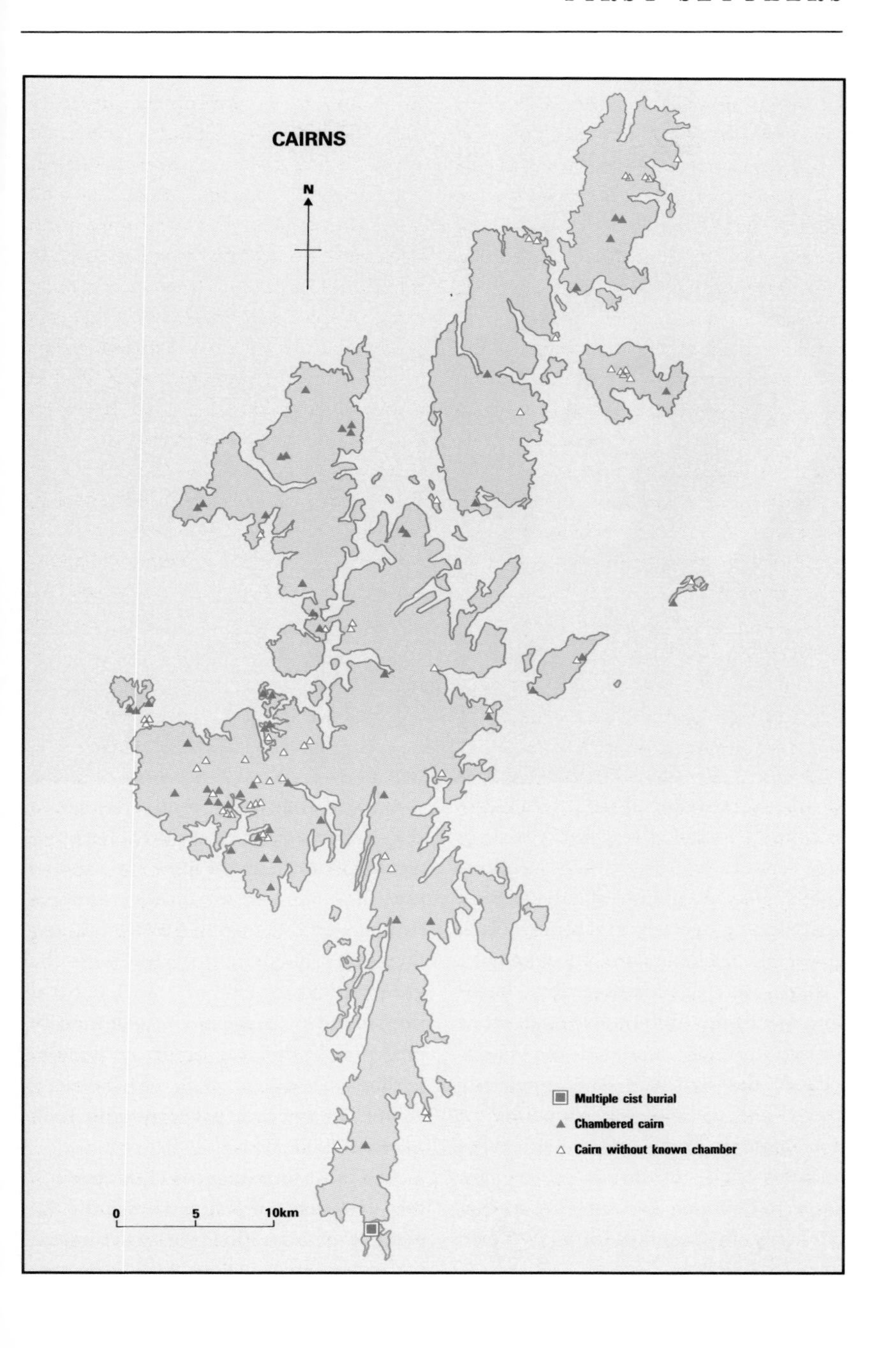
CAIRNS
N
Multiple cist burial
Chambered cairn
Cairn without known chamber
0
5
10km

The Stanydale hall from the air.
Photo: J. Dewar

by six internally. Finds from the excavation included fragments of very large pottery vessels of late Neolithic type, smaller fragments of early Bronze Age "beaker" pottery and some tools of typical late Neolithic form. Most notable, perhaps, were two features. First, there were few of the ubiquitous rough stone artefacts normally associated with houses. Second, the structure was apparently roofed, and the roof was supported on two central posts of considerable thickness made of spruce, a tree not native to Scotland and growing at that time only in Scandinavia and North America.

Clearly, Stanydale, if not a temple in the strict sense, must have been an important structure of some sort, and its size, and the use of massive timbers (which would be rare as driftwood, and therefore valuable), together with the general absence of agricultural implements, suggests a community enterprise. Perhaps it is a temple, perhaps a village hall. Archaeology cannot as yet deal properly with such questions.

The most puzzling aspect of all is not the existence of Stanydale, but the absence of corresponding structures in any other area rich in early remains.

Stanydale is even more exceptional in the Neolithic than Mousa in the Iron Age.

Taking together the evidence of houses, farms and burial places, together with their associated cairns and dykes, it can be seen that the early farmers who peopled Shetland lived an orderly life. They apparently agreed land divisions, were well equipped with crops and domestic animals, and seem to have had a respect for at least some of their dead. Their chambered tombs and a structures such as Stanydale argue for a society organised sufficiently to make large building projects feasible, and this in turn gives support to the idea of some form of a ruling or directing class.

Archaeology cannot demonstrate whether this class gained power through skill, knowledge, descent, martial prowess or some more esoteric advantage; once again, a tantalising problem seems insoluble, given the present skills of archaeology.

The Stanydale hall from its entrance, showing the side alcoves and the central post-holes. *Photo: D. Henrie*

ALTHOUGH the ruins of domestic and agricultural structures and burial places are the most obvious evidence of early settlement in Shetland, much of our knowledge has been gained from the study of tools, utensils and ornaments, items which archaeologists group under the name "artefacts", meaning objects fashioned by the art of man. While many features of early architecture in Shetland are hard to parallel exactly elsewhere, comparison of artefacts allows us to suggest links with other parts of the north. Before the invention of radiocarbon dating, these objects provided the only reasonably accurate means of dating the different phases of prehistory. The well-known "Three Ages" system: Stone Age, Bronze Age and Iron Age, and its subsequent finer subdivision, makes a useful framework for study on a local basis. However, is now realised that such divisions are never hard and fast, particularly in areas such as Shetland, far from the regions of southern Britain where these periods were first applied after their invention in Denmark.

The materials available elsewhere in Britain were all available to Shetlanders. There was ample clay for pottery, stone was abundant (including types which could be split and polished), wood was locally available, at least in pieces large enough to make tools, and bone would have been plentiful in the semi-pastoral economy which has always been practised in the islands. Added to these relatively long-surviving materials were such impermanent substances as leather, heather and straw. Anyone who doubts the importance of the last two items should examine the range of items made from them in recent times, in the Shetland Museum in Lerwick. Study of recent northern societies, such as the Inuit of Greenland and Northern Canada, shows great sophistication in the knowledge and use of the qualities of different types of animal hide and bird skin. And, Shetland being Shetland, we can assume that wool quickly became an important product, and would have provided most of the everyday clothing of the inhabitants.

Because of the poor conditions for preservation, only stone, pottery, some bone and a little wood survive from these pre-metal-using times. These are the materials which are found in excavations, and as chance finds. It is necessary to remember that all of the artefacts we study have survived the intervening millennia, and must, to be noticed,be recognisably manmade. This means we are looking at only a portion of the equipment of the well-provided Neolithic Shetlander,for we cannot study what has been destroyed, nor what has gone unnoticed. Many of the objects collected have been made with more care than was necessary for utility alone, and may therefore have had values in excess of the purely functional. There can be no doubt that there were, in the Neolithic as now, disposable tools; pebbles split to provide a sharp edge to gut a fish, or bones splintered to bore holes in leather or wood. Such items are not normally found, for they can only be identified by microscopic examination, and this cannot be carried out on every fragment recovered from an archaeological excavation or found by chance.

Pottery is very important in archaeological studies, because changing styles can help to assign sites to specific periods. All Shetland's prehistory pottery is hand-made, for the potter's wheel does not seem to have been introduced here until recently. Early pottery was made by building up coils of clay upon a flat base, and then smoothing the pot before decoration and firing. It tends to be gritty and coarse, and when broken into sherds may pass unnoticed by the untrained eye. Vessels vary in size and form, but are basically the storage jars and bowls which would be useful around any farm kitchen. Some of the decorative motifs suggest links with Orkney, although Shetland pottery seems to have lost little time in developing a character of its own. So far as we know, Neolithic people in the islands did not make special vessels to accompany burials in cists or cairns. This was a practice which began later, perhaps between 2000 and 1500 BC, when the thin-walled, highly decorated vase forms called "beakers" appear as one of the indicators of the start of the Bronze Age.

Containers were also carved out of steatite, a fibrous rock which can be shaped with stone tools, although metal implements would have been more efficient. This rock occurs in a number of places in Shetland, notably at Catpund (129) in South Mainland, and was worked to produce carved vessels and ornaments. Small chips of steatite were used as a filler in pottery clays. An alternative name for steatite is soapstone, because of its greasy feel and shiny surface. These properties were attractive to early potters, for clay containing steatite can be polished to a high gloss. By the end of the Neolithic, pottery containing steatite was to be found many miles from the nearest rock outcrop, raising the question of whether it travelled by trade or through collection and whether it was moved in the form of raw rock or fired pots. There can be little doubt that all Neolithic Shetlanders were capable of obtaining access to the full range of resources of the islands, no matter where they lived.

While pottery can be hard to identify, especially when weathered, and bone and wooden artefacts, even if preserved, are similarly elusive, stone tools are often easy to recognise. Thus it is that the majority of chance finds from this period are stone artefacts. The earliest tools found in Shetland are very basic in concept. At Jarlshof (26), split pebbles were used as knives at the start of the occupation of the site, but these were accompanied by a whole range of tools made from the local slate, which splits readily to provide flat blanks which can be shaped as required. Some of the tool types are clearly recognisable, as saws, knives, choppers and chisels, for example. While effective when new, the edges of slate tools would have dulled quickly with use. Because the rock weathers rapidly it is often hard to recognise slate tools when possible examples are found at any distance away from sites where, because of known settlement, they are expected to occur. This rock-type was used to make crude tools for many centuries. Since the form of such objects changes little they are hard to date to any definite period. Although the best known examples come from Jarlshof, most sites with any suitable rock nearby show their own assemblage of rough but effective tools.

Tougher-grained sandstones which occur in many areas were also used to make implements. Two forms of implement are particularly widespread, the mattock and the plough-tip. Mattocks are elongate flattened tools, about thirty centimetres long, ten wide and three to four thick. They taper towards the ends, and the tips frequently have smoothed areas on one or both sides consistent with use as a digging implement, presumably attached to some form of handle. Plough-tips, or "ard-points" are bars of roughly circular section tapering towards one end, and showing wear all round the point. This suggests they were being pushed or pulled through the soil, as the working end of a wooden stilt plough, or "ard" of the type occasionally found preserved in bogs. Most remarkably, direct evidence for this form of cultivation was found at Kebister, north of Lerwick, in the mid 1980s, when excavation of late Neolithic or early Bronze Age layers revealed the characteristic scratching of the sub-soil caused by this type of ploughing. While not in itself unique, similar evidence having been found at Sumburgh, the Kebister ard-marks in some cases ended in actual ard-shares embedded in the soil where they had broken on impact against stones.

Both types of artefact indicate cultivation of the ground, with the ard used to break up the soil when preparing the field, and the mattock used for everyday tilling. The large number of these objects littered around the cairns and walls associated with early houses suggests that they were a readily-made and disposable commodity, and in fact even the advent of iron did not banish the stone plough-tip, for examples were still in use into the early nineteenth century.

One further sandstone artefact type exists, and continues to puzzle experts. This is the "Shetland club". A number of heavy bars of smoothed sandstone, from thirty to eighty centimetres long, of variable thickness with an oval cross-section, have been found as stray finds during ploughing. These sometimes look rather like clumsy cricket-bats in shape, and may be decorated with simple incised lines. They look rather like clubs, hence their name, but would be awkward to hold and very ineffective as a weapon. Their purpose remains unknown, and since none has ever been found in an excavated context there remains some doubt about their date.

Sandstone served well enough for tools which did not need to be very sharp, or to have a long life, but was not suitable for many purposes. In particular, it could not produce razor-sharp cutting edges, or long-lasting scrapers for preparing hides, or points for arrows. Nor could heavy woodworking tools be made from sandstone. In most parts of Europe flint was used to produce finer types of artefact. Flint is a form of quartz resembling an impure glass, and can be flaked to produce a wide variety of shapes with sharp edges where required. Unfortunately for the Shetlanders, it has a very localised distribution, and does not occur in the islands except as small beach pebbles, which are often flawed and unsuitable for delicate shaping. By contrast, for heavier sharp tools, which were polished rather than flaked, Shetland was well-provided with the requisite material in the form of tough, close-grained igneous rock.

To overcome the lack of flint, prehistoric Shetlanders experimented with a variety of materials. The favourite, and that which was closest to flint, was quartz. This can produce sharp edges, but is much harder to work, for it is usually full of flaws which can cause it to crack in the wrong direction. Quartz tools are found, in the form of leaf-shaped arrowheads and small knives and scrapers, but these are generally not so elegant as their flint equivalents. A very few flint arrowheads are known, and these are probably of beach material. Since small fragments of quartz occur through the natural weathering of many of Shetland's rocks, quartz artefacts are less likely to be noticed than those of flint. Many years ago a magnificent axe of flint was found in Fair Isle (it is now in the National Museum of Scotland in Edinburgh) but this was probably imported as a manufactured object, since there is no record of flint pebbles large enough from any of the island beaches. No other comparable objects are recorded.

A smooth dark outcrop of porphyritic felsite at Beorgs of Uyea, which provided raw material for polished axes and knives. To its right is a roughly-roofed shelter of unknown date, and all around lie chippings and discarded flakes of rock.

The most characteristic tool-type of the Neolithic is the polished stone axe. Such axes are made by flaking a rough shape from a block of close-grained stone, then rubbing this down to produce a smooth, and sometimes highly polished, finish. The best rocks are hard volcanic ashes ("tuffs") and fine-grained intrusive igneous rocks; the latter are present in large quantities in North Mainland. Shetland has numerous examples of the two common polished tool types found in the rest of Britain, the axe and the mace-head, but it also has a unique type, found only in the islands, called the "Shetland knife".

All of these tools are easy to recognise, and are often noticed in fresh peat cuttings, where water on their smooth surfaces makes them glisten in the sunlight. Axes vary between ten and thirty centimetres in length, and are shaped like elongated and flattened pears, with the broader end ground to an axe-like edge. While tests have shown that such axes, when mounted in wooden hafts, are quite capable of cutting down trees, there is good evidence that they were valuable in their own right, and may have been made as much for show as for use. Similarly, mace-heads, which are again of varied sizes, could have been tools or weapons, but are often very ornate and carefully finished. Mace-heads are readily distinguished, as they have hafting holes bored through them. In shape, the Shetland examples are generally tapered cylinders, with the ends smoothed off. It is thought that mace-heads are later than axes, but both were in use together by the end of the Neolithic. The third artefact, the knife, is the most peculiar. Thin blocks of tough rock were flaked out and then ground from opposite sides to produce highly polished plates of oval shape and of thickness sometimes as little as four millimetres. These are in the order of fifteen to twenty centimetres long. When first made they seem to have had a sharp edge all round the circumference, but before use one of the long edges was ground smooth, to allow the knife to be held without cutting the hand or perhaps to be hafted without cutting into the haft and fixings. Such polished knives are not known outside Shetland, except for a single stray from Clydesdale, which may be a lost item from a recent antiquarian collection. While it may be that all of these highly polished tools were made as status symbols for their owners, there can be no doubt that some of them were used, for axes are found with chipped edges, and sometimes they have clearly been

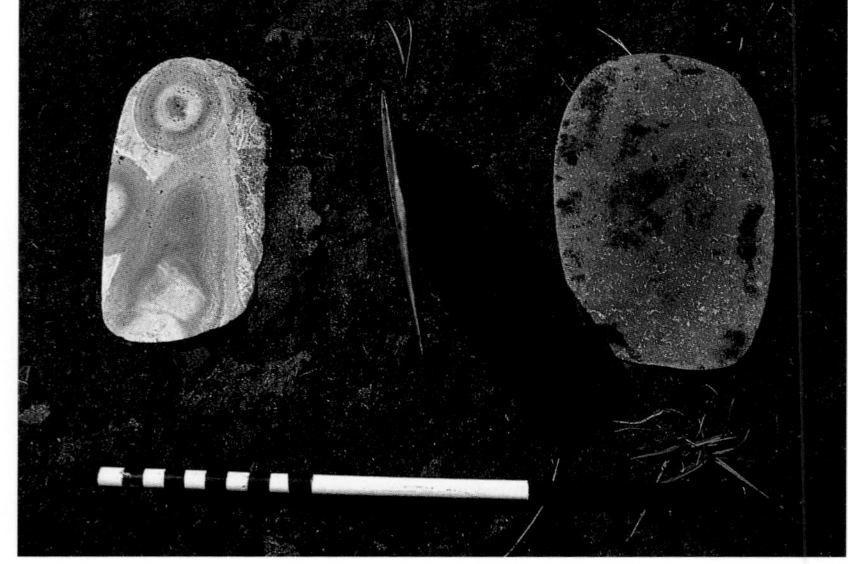

The end product: three polished stone knives (one turned on edge on to show its extreme thinness) just after their discovery in deep peat on Stourbrough Hill in 1978. The scale is 30cm long.

resharpened. Knives are also found in a wear-damaged state, and occasionally resharpened, both by chipping and grinding. Heavier knives tend to be roughly chipped into renewed sharpness, while the very slim, lightweight, forms are reground. But the majority of polished tools found in Shetland do not show obvious signs of wear. That these tools were intrinsically valuable is suggested by their occasional discovery in caches buried in peat. The locations of these hoards, and the fact that the artefacts are sometimes arranged in patterns, would suggest that these are offerings of some sort, and not just groups hidden or lost, or even buried in the peat as some part of the production process. One group of knives was found laid out in a circle, another arranged like books between two "bookends" of sandstone. Small groups of axes and larger groups of knives are occasionally found by peat cutters in areas far from even prehistoric habitations, and this suggests ritual deposition: for all we know, these may be offerings to appease the peat, which by the late Neolithic had begun to spread and cover the upper farmland. By a fortunate chance, many Shetland polished artefacts are of a rare rock. This is a speckled or banded felsite, an intrusive igneous rock, which occurs only in small outcrops on the northern slopes of North Mainland, beyond Ronas Hill. So objects made of rock from these outcrops can be recognised anywhere they occur. Axes and mace-heads of this particular felsite occur in other parts of Scotland, and even northern England, while knives are restricted to Shetland, suggesting the latter had a specialised use or appeal. More interesting still is that, within Shetland, axes and mace-heads made of non-Shetland stone have been recognised, including one from Sullom made of rock from the great axe factories at Langdale, in the English Lake District. Yet no knives have ever been found made of rocks which could not be of local origin, the vast majority coming from the felsites of North Mainland. This surely means that there was trade, or exchange, which was either to obtain axes, or used axes as a means of currency, while knives were only valued in Shetland, so did not usually leave the islands, whether as gifts or as payment. Some years ago, a shelter made of large granite blocks was found on the Beorgs of Uyea, west of North Roe (5). Inside this shelter, and all around it, were fragments of felsite, many of which had clearly been struck by the hand of man, and some of which looked like roughed-out axes and knives which had been abandoned part-way through, because of accidental breakage or the discovery of poor quality inclusions. The shelter itself had been made by roofing a hollow left where prehistoric man had dug down beside a large mass of the best quality rock, although it is not certain that the roofing is itself of prehistoric date. Since then several simpler working places have been found in the same area. It seems that the rock was quarried and roughly shaped on site, and then taken away for final polishing. The evidence for this is the occasional occurrence of unpolished rough-outs far away from the outcrop, and the absence of broken or whole polished artefacts at the working areas themselves. It is unfortunate that few polished implements have been found in datable contexts. There are fragments of knives from sites as late as brochs, but these may well have been found by chance then, as they are still sometimes found today, introducing the interesting concept of Iron Age antiquarianism: we know that Iron Age individuals collected exotic items from outside their immediate locality, for many Roman finds occur in Orkney brochs, having presumably been acquired as loot or trade goods. Some prehistoric houses have produced tools made by chipping rather than grinding this rock-type, and from the house at Stanydale came a much re-sharpened miniature axe. Only one excavation produced both knives and axes together, but this, at Modesty in West Mainland, took place before the days of radiocarbon dating, and we know little of the circumstances, except that pottery which may have been late Neolithic was found. It may well be that the actual production of knives and axes took place over a relatively short period at the end of the Neolithic and the beginning of the Bronze Age, and that the stock of implements was then gradually reduced by breakage, loss and use as votive offerings. The reason for suggesting a period of manufacture into the Bronze Age is that some Shetland axes closely resemble, in form, early flat bronze axes. It may be that this shape, an impractical one for stoneworking, represents an attempt to copy a new technology in old materials. By the early Iron Age, rock types once used to make polished implements were being used as substitutes for flint, and worked by chipping and flaking.

Before considering metallurgy, mention must be made of the huge gaps in our knowledge. Some bone tools of early date are known, notably awls, needles and chisels. In addition, pegs and toggles were made from bone, while larger bones were used, with little preparation, as shovels and mattocks. Ribs were sharpened and used as knives for cutting up blubber and meat. However, these tools survive only on a few sandy sites, for elsewhere they have dissolved in the acid soils which cover most of Shetland. Early wooden tools doubtless existed in great number and variety, but these too have vanished, although a few objects survive from the Iron Age and later. One major source of materials may have been whales, for as well as providing food, a whale provides oil and bone. Inuit tents of recent times had their roofs supported by whale ribs, and these may have been put to similar use in early Shetland. Whale vertebrae are large enough to form seats, or working platforms for stone-chipping. There can be no doubt that if whales, then more plentiful than now, were stranded on Shetland shores then the thrifty Neolithic inhabitants would have been able to make good use of their unexpected bounty. With all these skills in artefact manufacture available, it would hardly be surprising to learn that Shetland quickly adopted metallurgy when knowledge of bronze arrived, around 1800 BC.

In fact, the opposite is true, for there is very little evidence for early bronze-working in Shetland, nor are early types of bronze artefact known. It is not until the end of the Bronze Age, around 700 BC or later, that we find evidence for metal-working at the long established site of Jarlshof, and also at Wiltrow, a nearby house site. Nor were bronze objects imported in any quantity into Shetland from sources outside the islands, for the sole example of a bronze weapon remains one splendid spearhead found many years ago in Lunnasting. But this need not mean that bronze was not imported, or worked, at this period. However, since Shetland was by this time becoming more impoverished because of climatic deterioration, the wherewithal of trade may have been limited, and Shetland lies far from the nearest sources. There are copper veins in the islands, but there is no proof that these were known at this early date. It seems likely that bronze would have been a precious commodity, not to be wasted or lost, and that scrap fragments and outmoded or outworn tools would have been carefully gathered for reworking into more useful forms. A practice of recycling would help to explain the observation that at the end of the Bronze Age the evidence for use of bronze increases markedly, to the extent that the early Iron Age of Shetland is marked by an increase in the amount of bronze found on sites. Bronze, now less valuable than the new metal, iron, might have been treated less carefully, leaving more for archaeologists to discover in future years.

From the later Bronze Age we know of two smiths' workshops, both producing ornaments and a few weapons. As well as scrap bronze and slag, fragments of moulds have been found at both sites, together with crucibles. The style of the artefacts being produced dates firmly to the period just before the introduction of iron working, and although it has been suggested that these are the products of immigrant smiths who were reluctant to change their accustomed bronze to iron, and so moved north with their obsolescent trade, this seems rather unlikely. There were perfectly good uses for bronze which did not require iron, and bronze is of course used in modern times: iron did not supplant bronze, it simply supplemented it. The start of the Iron Age seems to be associated with changes in society, a more restless and troubled period, and this may in itself have been the cause of an increase in the need for weapons. Some artefacts, such as swords, may have been made of bronze for much of the Iron Age, until iron-working techniques developed to rival those of the bronze-smiths. In addition, the Iron Age ushered in changes in building styles, with larger and more elaborage constructions, using large quantities of wood and presumably requiring more heavy tools such as saws and adzes. The bone handles of such metal tools have been recovered from early Iron Age levels at Clickimin (22). Having now, in pursuit of early technology, come far ahead of our time, we must return to the late Neolithic to observe the way in which society was gradually changing.

ALTHOUGH bronze itself is scarce, many of the changes associated with the first use of bronze elsewhere do occur in Shetland, which can thus be said to have a Bronze Age. New trends can be seen in stone artefacts, in burial practices, in pottery and in the location of settlements. During the Bronze Age, which is usually dated to the period 1800 to 600 BC, a widespread new class of site, the burnt mound, appears.

The key to this period is the climatic change which seems to have started in the later Bronze Age in southern Scotland, but was apparently earlier in the north. From 1500 BC, or a little later, the climate changed to a wetter and cooler regime, a trend which continued for over a thousand years. New evidence from excavations in Shetland, particularly at Kebister, is beginning to suggest that the climatic changes may have coincided with, and possibly been partly caused by, a series of violent volcanic eruptions in Iceland in the mid to late second millennium BC. The evidence for this takes the form of extremely thin layers of volcanic dust interleaved with peat and soil deposits. It has been suggested that large quantities of such dust, blown high into the atmosphere, could in themselves result in a cooling effect and a reduction in direct sunlight.

By the Bronze Age querns were becoming smaller and are less frequent finds on excavated sites: these are at Jarlshof.

Whatever the causes, for Shetland, already on the margins of arable cultivation, the result of this climatic change was that peat began to accumulate on the higher ground, especially where the soil may have been exhausted by continual cropping without proper manuring. As time went by this blanket of peat grew further and further downslope, burying the Neolithic farmland, and ultimately many of the habitations of the farmers. This was fortunate for archaeologists, but a disaster for the inhabitants of Shetland, who must have found themselves gradually forced down from the hill slopes to the areas around the voes, which would have been well populated already. To add to this overcrowding, the slow rise of the sea was inundating low-lying land around the shore, particularly in areas such as Virkie, where the gentle offshore slope meant that a slight rise in sea-level would destroy considerable tracts of flat land.

The farmers made the best they could of this situation, adapting to become more dependent upon their domesticated animals, and less upon crops. Probably the resources of the sea began to be exploited more fully at this time, although in worsening weather conditions this may not have been easy.

The effects of cumulative changes in climate must have been severe: not only was the arable area reduced, but lower temperatures and more rain would have made crops less reliable, and would have helped to waterlog the fields, a process made worse by the trampling of cattle. By the latter part of the Bronze Age, around 1000 BC and later, there can be little doubt that Shetland was supporting more people than it could comfortably accommodate. The results of this were to be felt in the following period, the Iron Age.

If, as argued above, population density on the coastal lands built up during the Bronze Age, it may seem strange that there is so little in the way of evidence for Bronze Age settlement, as distinct from Neolithic, and that so few typically "Bronze Age" artefacts should have been discovered. However, this is readily explained. Since Shetland was becoming gradually less hospitable, inducements to new settlers would have been slight, and the existing inhabitants may well have been openly hostile to newcomers. This, coupled with a shortage of wealth to acquire bronze, would be sufficient to account for the lack of artefactual evidence for outside contacts during the second millennium BC. A few new

Bronze Age houses are often circular, as seen at Jarlshof (the group of foundations nearest the modern building in the right foreground).

One of the excavated Bronze Age houses at Jarlshof.

practices were acquired from occasional contacts with the south, but by and large the way of life was conservative, particularly in aspects such as house building, where a type of structure suited to the Shetland environment, once developed, stayed in vogue for over three thousand years, from the early farms of the Neolithic right through into the Iron Age. The only major building change is that circular houses seem gradually to have become more popular, and that house walls tend to become a little thinner. The end of this change can be seen in the houses at Jarlshof.

The only radical change in Shetland during the Bronze Age which might justify the idea of a new period was in funerary practices. Neolithic burials were inhumations, where the whole body was buried, rather than cremations. Burials were made in chambered cairns, in massive cists (with or without overlying cairns) and presumably into the earth alone, without elaborate preparations, and were generally multiple rather than single. In the Bronze Age, individual burial came to be prevalent in Shetland as elsewhere in Britain. With this new ritual came new types of pottery, in particular the open-mouthed, vase-like vessels called ''beakers'', a term which recent research has shown to be very apposite, for some beakers can be shown to have contained a drink akin to mead. Beakers are associated with the early Bronze Age, and generally accompany burials of unburned bodies which lie with their knees drawn up to their chins. Not many beaker burials are known from Shetland. Native potters seem to have adopted and adapted beakers to their own ends, and begun to produce a range of coarser vessels with beaker-like incised decorations and less elegant forms. These are classed as "food vessels", for no very good reason, and together with larger vessels termed "urns", are found on domestic sites, occurring at many of the oval houses, and are also found as the containers for cremations, the type of burial which becomes the mode in the later Bronze Age. Such urns are rather more frequent in Shetland than beakers, and tend to occur in the coastal areas where we assume most people lived.

The practice of burying large numbers of individuals in cairns ceases entirely shortly after the beaker pottery appears, and a further change occurred as urns replaced beakers and the burial rite became one of cremation, with the ashes placed in or under a pottery vessel. However, it may be that all forms of collective religion did not cease, for urn burials are frequently found in groups, while the hall at Stanydale has pottery from this period and, indeed, later.

Accompanying these changes in burial practices we find a change in one important artefact type, the arrowhead. While Neolithic arrows were tipped with pointed oval heads, made of flint or quartz (and in Shetland also of felsite), Bronze Age arrowheads are of the more familiar classic form, a sharp triangle with two barbs on either side of a protruding tang, which was fastened into the shaft of the arrow. These barbed and tanged arrowheads are very rare in Shetland, probably because they are very hard to fabricate from quartz, since they require delicate flaking which only flint allows at all readily. In all likelihood oval, or "leaf-shaped", arrowheads of quartz carried on in use throughout the Bronze Age.

A simple stone cist below a cairn was the commonest form of burial in the Bronze Age: in this example, at Pettigarths Field, Whalsay, the cist is below an expansion of a small, earlier, chambered cairn.

A few other artefact types, known only from stray finds, have been singled out as of Bronze Age date, on evidence from elsewhere in Britain. Amongst these are the mace-heads mentioned above, and some of the rather puzzling objects called "Shetland clubs" may also be of this date. There is also evidence that some Shetland knives carried on in use, and indeed may have been manufactured, during the Bronze Age. In fact, it appears that the introduction of bronze was not, as is sometimes casually believed, accompanied by a decrease in the quantity or standard of stone-working. In fact certain artefacts, such as arrowheads, seem to have improved, almost as if they were trying to compete with the new material. Thus the polished stone axes of the Neolithic were also produced in the Bronze Age, but in forms which emulated the new bronze axes.

During the Bronze Age, a new class of monument appeared. This was the "burnt mound". Most examples are kidney-shaped in plan and are, as their name implies, large mounds of fire-reddened and cracked stones. The stones are generally small, pebble to cobble sized. On excavation, these mounds have been shown to possess troughs made of flat slabs of stone, and traces of hearths are frequently found, with fragments of coarse pottery and sometimes bone. More rarely, small houses of wood or stone have been found close beside, and partly buried in, burnt mounds. There is little doubt that these monuments represent the cooking places of people who did not possess pottery vessels large enough to boil large joints of meat and who had devised an

Kidney-shaped or dented oval in plan, and always near water: a burnt mound at Niddister, Hillswick.

ingenious escape from the monotony of roasted food. The central trough would be filled with water (all mounds lie close to fresh water sources), a fire kindled on the hearth and stones placed in it to heat. A joint of meat was then placed in the trough, and the water in this brought to boiling point by adding hot stones, perhaps with the aid of a bone shovel. The temperature could be maintained by adding stones from time to time, until the meat was cooked. Experiments have shown that this procedure is slow but effective. The presence of sherds of coarse pottery suggests that other foods were prepared to accompany the main item on the menu. As well as joints of meat, other economical dishes could be made from left-overs mixed with vegetables or grain. For example haggis would be ideally suited to this culinary method.

The stone trough at the heart of each burnt mound held heated water: Burnside, Hillswick.

In some cases whole houses, of the usual oval plan, have been found part-

Burnt mounds can be very small: Vaasetter, Fair Isle . . .

buried in these mounds, and this might imply that trough-boiling was a normal method of cooking, and not something indulged in only for occasional feasts. On the other hand, it may be that this seemingly simple change to the preparation of large quantities of food at one time marks a much deeper trend in late Bronze Age Shetland, a trend which intensified in the Iron Age.

. . . or very large: Houlalie, on Fair Isle, is probably Scotland's largest burnt mound.

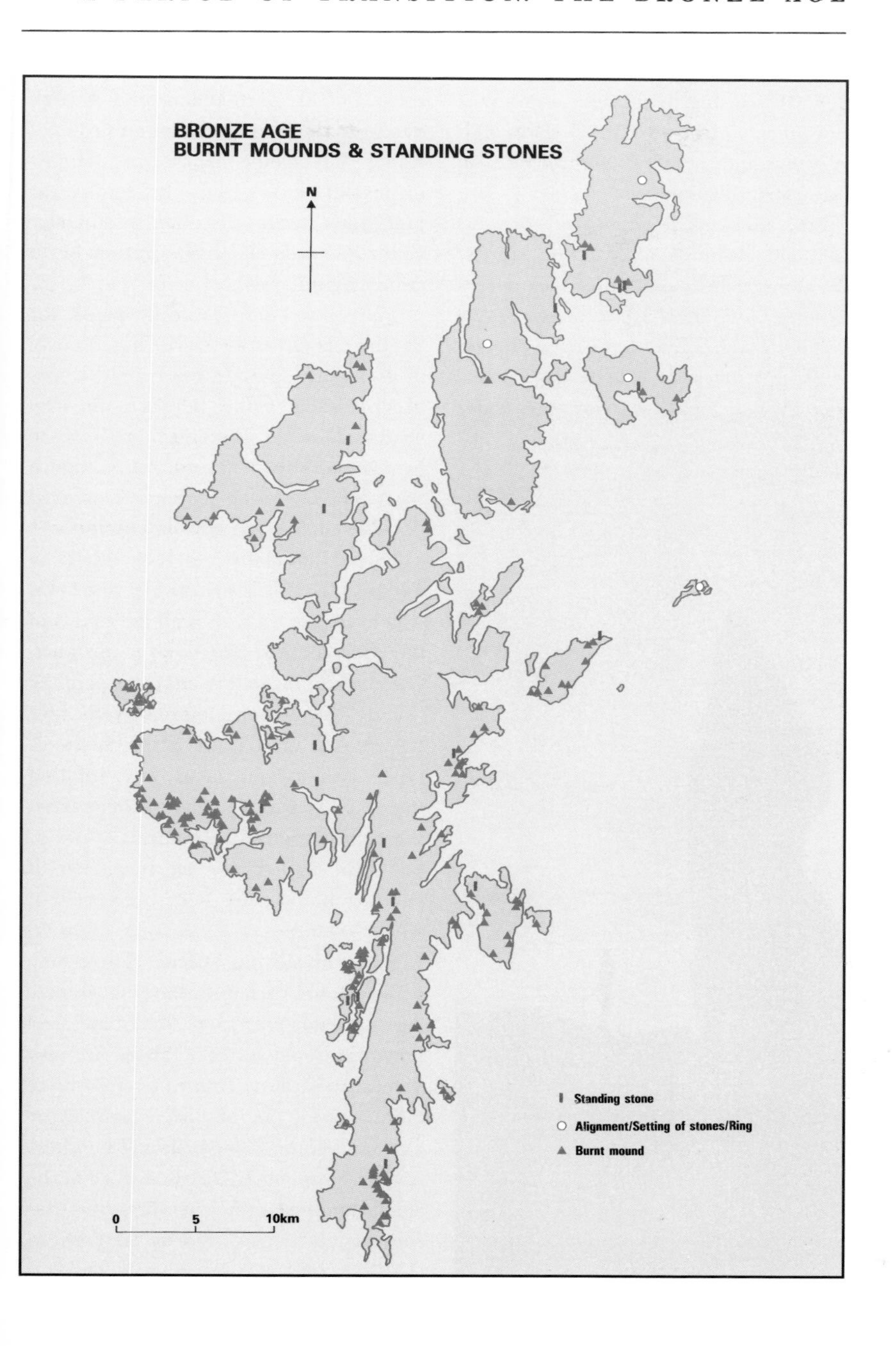
BRONZE AGE
BURNT MOUNDS & STANDING STONES
N
Standing stone
Alignment/Setting of stones/Ring
Burnt mound
0
5
10km

STONES ON END

BEFORE moving on to the Iron Age, it is worth pausing to consider a group of monuments which are hard to place, both in time and in their significance to prehistoric Shetlanders.

Like most parts of upland Britain, Shetland abounds in standing stones, often single but sometimes laid out in patterns. We know from other regions that such stones may have been erected at various dates, so it is perhaps better to look at them alone, rather than in the context of any particular period. Rough dates can be given to circles and rows of stone, but single blocks are almost impossible to place, especially as prehistoric stones were often used in later years as markers for navigation or to define boundaries.

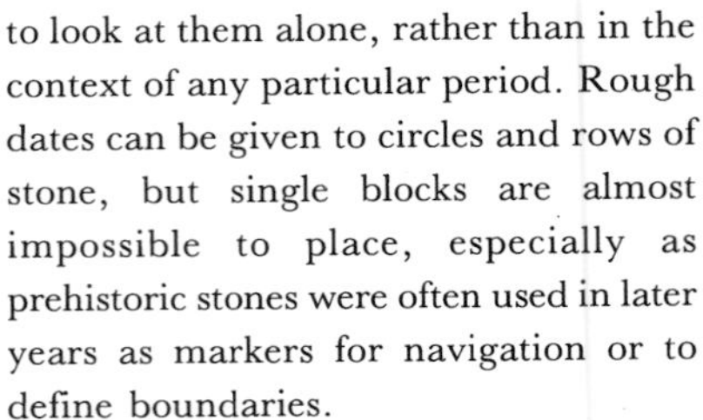

Dramatic landmark: "The Auld Wife" at Skellister, South Nesting.

The only "stone circle" listed for Shetland is rather unconvincing, an oval of irregularly spaced stones on the slopes of Wormadale Hill, between the new road and the old. It seems more likely to be the remains of an enclosure than a true, ritual, stone circle. A second possible circle is the puzzling monument called "Hjaltadans", on the moors of Fetlar (37). This is a ring of large blocks, which are not on end, with the centre of the circle marked by two large uprights. Once again, the date is unknown, but the "circle" bears some similarity to later Bronze Age burial cairns of the "kerbed" type, although it lacks any infilling material. To complete the trio of puzzles, there are the puzzling Rounds of Tivla, on Unst (28). These are three sets of circular banks, the best preserved of which has three concentric rings of earth, with a central stony spread. These may be a regional variant of the later Bronze Age burial tradition of "enclosed cremation cemeteries". There are also several irregularly shaped enclosures of large stones, the best of which is the Battle Pund, on Out Skerries (43). These may be simply large fields with all of the small stones from the walls removed, but this has yet to be tested by excavation.

While circular settings can, in general,

be fitted into a late Neolithic or Bronze Age range of dates, the stone rows of northern Scotland are much harder to place. These are settings of small, upright, stones arranged in parallel or slightly diverging lines. The best example so far known from Shetland was discovered recently in central Yell. Three rows of stubby uprights, running parallel and oriented north-east to south-west, lie on a flattish area beside the Loch of Lumbister (35). They are crossed by a shorter row of larger blocks, which is aligned north to south. This is not nearly so spectacular as some of the examples known from Caithness, such as Hill o'Many Stanes at Mid Clyth, but it is equally inexplicable, at least until an example has been excavated. Expert guesses have placed these monuments in the earlier part of the Bronze Age, purely on the frequently observed association with other classes of monument.

Most of the upright stones of Shetland occur singly. They are very difficult to date, but there can be little doubt that some may go back to the late Neolithic. Stone uprights have been used for many purposes over the years, especially in an area with no large trees, and there is no reason why a Neolithic standing stone should not be a boundary mark, or a

Ruined cairn: the two standing stones beside the road at Housetter, North Roe, are the terminals of the facade of a robbed-out cairn.

Photo: S. White

Bronze Age monolith a navigation point. Whatever the motives behind their erection, all standing stones furnish useful landmarks in a landscape of generally undistinguished relief.

Many Neolithic heel-shaped cairns had an orthostat (an upright earthfast block) set at each outer end of the facade, and when cairns have been robbed for building material, it is often only these orthostats, which were too large to carry, which are left. A good example of this can be seen at Housetter, beside the road to North Roe (44). Sometimes pairs of stones are quite clearly set so as to provide markers for entering difficult harbours; the pair at Clivocast (32), near Uyeasound, would fall into this class. Even single stones often seem to be set so as to act as sailing marks, for example the stones at Busta (51), or at Feal in Fetlar (38). Still more of the standing stones of Shetland are quite clearly markers used in defining boundaries, and this practice of setting up stones to mark corners of landholdings was continued into the medieval period, although its origins lie far earlier, as shown by the discovery, many years ago, of a set of stone knives buried near a standing stone at Wester Skeld (61). Surprisingly, considering the grim legends often associated with standing stones and stone circles, no one has ever found a burial associated with a Shetland stone.

So single stones must remain enigmatic, for they are known to have been erected at every period and for every purpose. Even in modern times, the impulse to raise stones remains, as may be seen by the examples beside many stretches of new road. Fortunately for the archaeologist, these tend to bear the date of their erection. Settings of multiple stones, however, are most likely to be of Bronze Age date.

THE middle part of the first millennium BC saw a major change in Shetland. From unenclosed single farms of the Neolithic and early Bronze Age there gradually evolved more nucleated settlements, with houses clustered together, often close to the shore, as at Jarlshof. As already described, there were good environmental reasons for this, but at some time in the later Bronze Age a new factor emerged, that of self-defence.

Since the number of people was gradually increasing while the capacity of the land to carry those numbers was decreasing, it was inevitable that in Shetland, as elsewhere in northern and western Europe, the time would come when minor wrangles over territory would develop into longer lasting feuds, and feuds into localised warfare. To find protection from hostile neighbours, bands of families would have joined together, and slowly leaders would have emerged to direct operations in times of trouble. This emergence of communities with close ties and identifiable leaders, while helping to protect the individual, led ultimately to more instability, for the new organisation of society allowed raids and land-takings which were impossible under the older system where social co-operation appears to have been based more upon religious than military needs, and structured accordingly.

It would be naive to imagine this happened in Shetland without any outside influences, and certainly the first signs of defensive structures are close in time to the arrival of new styles of pottery, new bronze ornaments and, most important, a new metal, iron. There is much debate as to how these introductions are related to the wider changes in society. It has been argued that all the new traits, plus the idea of building fortifications, arrived with settlers from the south, presumably Orkney. But the evidence is not conclusive. At Clickimin, a fort was built before the first traces of iron-working appear; at Jarlshof, the reverse seems to be true, while at Wiltrow iron was worked in a house which is in every appearance an ordinary domestic dwelling of Neolithic-Bronze Age type.

It is perhaps safest to state that iron arrived at approximately the same period as a major reorganisation of society over the whole of northern Scotland, including Shetland. This reorganisation took the form of the clustering of families into larger units, which in turn brought forth a stratification in society, with certain individuals or families emerging as leaders of their communities. This reorganisation made possible a more territorial approach to inter-community relationships, and allowed major projects of defensive construction to be undertaken. The results have come down to us in the form of the ruins of many forts and brochs.

It is unlikely that some sort of organising hierarchy was new: after all, the chambered cairns, or Stanydale hall, were considerable feats, probably requiring strong central direction. The major change in the early Iron Age (around 500 BC), is that the direction is towards defence, and that a large number of sizeable projects seem to have been undertaken in a relatively short space of time. The nucleation of society helped to reinforce the trends of slow response to the changes in the climate, so that the distribution of population in Shetland changed from a scatter all around the coasts to a series of coastal units, each centred on a single site, where a defensive structure had been erected.

It is often thought that the only common type of fortified dwelling in the north of Scotland is the broch, a tall circular fort with a thick, hollow wall and a single small entrance. Recent work has shown that, while brochs are still numerically dominant, other types of fort are not nearly so rare as has been assumed. So far there is no firm evidence for the relative dating of brochs and other types of defence, although the fort at Clickimin clearly predated the broch there by many years. The form of some forts seems to be pre-broch in conception, while others may be broadly contemporary with the brochs.

Shetland's non-broch forts are all relatively small in area, and occur in two kinds of location: on cliffed promontories and on small islands in lochs or sheltered voes. Both types of site made possible the enclosure of an adequate area with a minimum of work. A whole promontory could be cut off with a short wall across the neck, while on defended islets approached by narrow causeways it is

Earthen ramparts and ditches at the Landberg promontory fort on Fair Isle.

usually observed that the walling is heavy only on the side of the islet nearest the causeway, and much slighter elsewhere around the circuit. This may be seen at Loch of Huxter, Whalsay (98).

Defences were constructed in quite a variety of ways, including simple stone walls, stone-faced earthen ramparts and ramparts of earth alone. All types of defence (with ditches on some, but not all, sites) tend not to be very substantial. Even the earthen ramparts seldom exceed ten metres in breadth, and may have been no more than three metres high. However, this would have been quite adequate to turn the natural awkwardness of a well-chosen site into a reliable defence. Most forts are simple in concept. Promontory ramparts run across the narrowest part of a neck of land, usually leaving a narrow gap at one side or the other, which we must assume was closed by a gate of wood. Good examples of these simple forts are widespread, and particularly fine specimens can be seen at Aywick (Yell) (94) and Ness of Garth (Sandness) (102). At the last named and at Hog Island Sound, in North Nesting (101), rising sea-level has made islands of what were probably promontories when the forts were built.

Ramparts are generally simple elongate mounds of earth and stones, sometimes with an external facing of masonry. However, some sites were enclosed by stout stone walls, and it is likely that many apparently earthen ramparts are formed by the collapse of stone walls. This was seen at Scatness

The fort at Stoal, Aywick, Yell, occupies a typical rocky promontory.

Photo: M. Brooks

At Hog Island Sound the sea has cut away the original approach to the fort.

Photo: M. Brooks

(110), where a stone blockhouse was found on excavation to have broken down so that it formed a sloping bank. Forts on islets generally have a stone wall, from one to three metres thick, running around the edge, with a single narrow entrance. Good examples can be seen from the road at Loch of Brindister and Burga Water (100), and further afield at Loch of Kettlester, in Yell, and Loch of Huxter, in Whalsay.

At Loch of Huxter, the wall was built onto the ends of an elaborate gateway,

Seen shortly after excavation in 1983, the fort at Scatness displays a combination of blockhouse and rampart.

Photo: M. Brooks

The classic blockhouse fort at Ness of Burgi.

which ran across the side of the islet nearest the shore and the approach causeway. This consisted of a rectangular block of masonry with an entrance passage running through it, and contained two basal cells. Above this level was a hollow gallery, running within the wall thickness, which would have given any defender a height advantage over an attack from outside. The entrance, cells and hollow wall are features also found in brochs, and they are repeated in similar "blockhouses" at Ness of Burgi (111), Scatness and Clickimin, while ruined examples occur at Burgi Geos (Yell) (92) and, probably, at Burraland broch, opposite Mousa.

These elaborate forts show broch-like features, but it has so far proved impossible to say whether they are ancestral to the brochs or simply contemporary adaptations for peculiar situations. The evidence from Clickimin suggests an early date for the blockhouse there, and this evidence, together with the West Burrafirth broch, which looks like an experiment in hollow wall construction, leads one to think that here may be one of the various drystone building traditions which were amalgamated to produce that most studied of Scottish fortifications, the broch.

Before discussing brochs, it should be noted that about half of the seventy-five examples in Shetland have ramparts or walls outside the broch tower itself, and some of these are in fact substantial enough to have served as defences in their own right. But for the presence of the broch, the outer defences at sites such as Burland (105), Aithsetter and Burraland would fall into the class of promontory forts, and would be by no means the slightest of these. Away from the coast, a number of brochs are surrounded by walls reminiscent of the early fort at Clickimin: Culswick (104) and Southpunds (107) are fine examples. Substantial series of earthen ramparts surround brochs such as Underhoull on Unst (89), Belmont, on the same island (90), and Dalsetter, in South Mainland (109). So on at least some sites, the broch may not be the first defence to have been erected, and this suggests that there may be a much longer history of conflict in Iron Age Shetland than has hitherto been realised.

Although the brochs are the best known of Shetland's prehistoric remains, surprisingly little can be said with certainty about their inhabitants or the circumstances of their construction, for there have been very few modern excavations, and old digging did not produce very much information, since it

Stout ramparts surround the mound of the ruined broch of Dalsetter.

Photo: M. Brooks

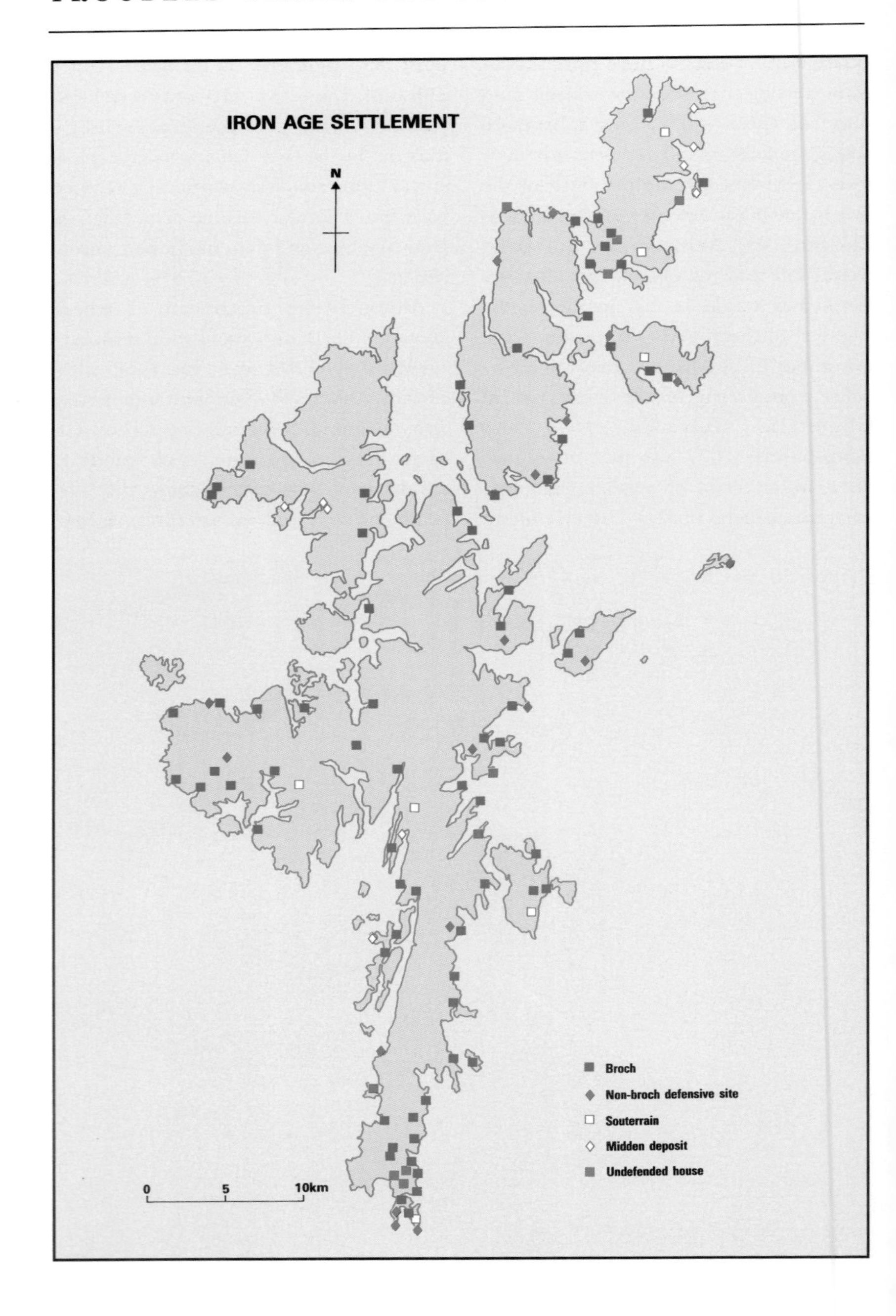
IRON AGE SETTLEMENT
N
0
5
10km
Broch
Non-broch defensive site
Souterrain
Midden deposit
Undefended house

concentrated upon the search for artefacts and tended to ignore details of construction and the organic remains which can now be studied to help reconstruct the economy of times past. Recent work in Orkney has revealed that structures which may be early fortifications, ancestral to brochs, were being built there as early as 600 BC. Many of the Shetland brochs show considerable similarity one to another, and this tends to support the idea that the majority were built over a short space of time, perhaps two centuries at most. The most likely picture is a slow process of development, with few brochs being built, as problems were ironed out, followed by a rapid spread of the structural type once a workable design had evolved.

Shetland possesses, on the island of Mousa (106), the best preserved broch anywhere in Scotland. A circular foundation, four and a half metres thick, surrounds an inner courtyard six metres in diameter. This massive foundation is pierced by an entrance passage a little over one metre wide, with a recess partway along it to take the frame of a now-vanished wooden door. Within the solid wallbase are three oval cells with corbelled roofs. These are reached from

Mousa broch survives to its original height of over 13 metres.

From the air, Mousa's hollow-walled construction is evident.
Photo: J. Dewar

the inner court through narrow passages. Three metres above ground level the character of the broch wall changes, and from this height upwards it is hollow, with six level galleries, each one floored by the lintels which roof the gallery below. A steep stairway spirals upwards within this hollow wall, cutting through the galleries, to emerge at the wallhead thirteen metres above the ground and probably close to the full original height of the broch. Within the court may have stood wooden tenements, supported on central posts and on the ledges of stone which protrude from the inner face of the broch. These, and their roof, have long vanished, and the sockets which would have held their supporting posts have been concealed by stone fittings on the floor of the broch. Such wooden platforms would have allowed a sizeable number of people to shelter inside the tower but might equally well have been used for more everyday functions such as storing hay.

While Mousa looks almost too good to be true, there seems to be no truth in the often-heard story that it is a nineteenth-century reconstruction, although it was repaired around 1851. It was well enough preserved in the eleventh century to serve as a shelter for Norse fugitives. However,

Mousa is not quite representative of the majority of Shetland's more ruined brochs. Having a smaller diameter and a more massive wall than most, Mousa probably stands higher than almost any other broch ever did, but there is little doubt that many brochs were tall enough to be described as towers. Mousa also lacks the ingenious guard cells found in most other brochs. These are small cells with their narrow entrances opening into the main entrance passage just behind the door recess, in such a fashion that a single man stationed in the guard cell could obstruct the passage of many, as they would be forced to enter in single file. Another pitfall awaiting the unwary visitor was an arrangement whereby spaces were left between the lintels which roof the passage, so that a man in the gallery above could see, and spear, any unwelcome guest. This can be seen to advantage at Clickimin.

Of the seventy-five likely brochs in Shetland, enough are sufficiently preserved to enable us to say that Mousa is a very solid, and possibly late, example. It seems almost to be an exhibition of the capabilities of the builders, for its height is wholly excessive to any defensive requirements, especially as the absence of guard cells or strong outer ramparts argues against the idea that it was intended as a very strongly defensible structure.

Most brochs in Shetland had a number of lesser buildings outside them. It may be that at some brochs these buildings were in use at the same time as the brochs, and served to house members of a group which had grown too large for everyone to live permanently within the

The massive triangular lintel of the granite-built Culswick broch.

Inside Clickimin a chamber above the entrance passage reduced the weight of the wall and provided a useful view down into the passage.

Not all brochs were built on new sites: this small house at Clickimin dates from the late Bronze Age, and was used by the broch-builders while they worked on their new defence.

tower. At other sites, it can clearly be seen that the external remains are those of houses which post-date both broch and outer defences, as at Snabrough (Unst) and Loch of Houlland (Eshaness) (99). At both of theses sites the houses lie over the ruins of the brochs. At Clickimin and Jarlshof some of the external dwellings have been shown to be earlier than the brochs, and a similar situation probably occurs at Southpunds. Little systematic study has been devoted to such remains in Shetland, but it appears that large numbers of subsidiary houses do seem to occur where the local land is of above average quality.

What were the brochs ? They appear to have developed as strongly-built farmhouses, with internal arrangements capable of temporarily housing large numbers of people. The ancestors of brochs can be found in the early forts and roundhouses of Orkney and Shetland, the ''wags'' of Caithness and, perhaps, the galleried duns and promontory forts of the Hebrides. These all contributed elements to the eventual broch design, which can thus be seen as a mingling of the skills of the whole of Scotland's northern Atlantic seaboard. The brochs were passively defensive, with only the wallhead available as a fighting platform, from which weapons and stones could be hurled, but only at the risk of silhouetting oneself against the sky and making an easy target for an attacker with a ready spear. It seems that the builders of brochs feared for their own lives rather than for their property, for the internal space of brochs is inadequate to accommodate the chief resource of these farmers, their cattle. Also, the attackers cannot have been much stronger in military terms than the defenders, for the expedient of simply running inside and shutting the door seems to have been deemed sufficient defence. The Romans, had they reached these parts, would have made short work of a broch. The type of society behind broch building was most likely one where feuding and raiding played a major part, with the unhappy losers being sold into slavery elsewhere.

An alternative, or partial alternative, view is that most brochs were probably never put to the test. The broch may well have been a fad, a way of demonstrating the prestige of a group, or of a group's leaders. Since it took time to build, and time was of value then as now, there may have been great esteem to be gained from showing how much spare time the group had: an early form of communal status

Burland broch at Brindister stands close to tall cliffs, adding natural defensibility.

symbol. There seems to be no other way of explaining Mousa's excessive height, or the elaboration of outer ramparts at Belmont.

Compared with broch architecture, the life of brochs' inhabitants has received scant attention. From a study of the places in which brochs are found, we can infer that they represent the homes of groups of farmers who practised a mixed economy, but with an emphasis on cereal growing which seems more in tune with the earlier Neolithic than the immediately preceding Bronze Age. This was to some extent made possible by a stabilisation in the climate after the long period of worsening conditions experienced through the Bronze Age, but was largely the inevitable consequence of the formation of larger groups of inhabitants. The Iron Age saw the start of the pattern of land use familiar to the present day, with a small settlement nucleus surrounded by well-manured arable with good grazing land behind, merging into moorland. And doubtless the farmers then, as earlier and later, took advantage of the bounty of the sea, especially when harvests were poor. Because the Iron Age farmer used the same land, in much the same way, as later Shetlanders, it is hard to find evidence of their fields, but a few

This early twentieth-century hand-powered rotary quern, for grinding corn, remains essentially unchanged in design from its middle Iron Age predecessor.

traces can be seen around Greenbank on Yell and also at the nearby Burra Ness (93). Clearance cairns of probable Iron Age date can be seen at Burra Ness, at Belmont in Unst and near Burgi Geos, on the desolate west coast of northern Yell. These traces only survive where the land has proved too poor for subsequent farmers to have settled for long.

Some time around the latter half of the second century AD brochs seem to have gone out of fashion, either because the threat of violent attack had ceased, or because they simply became outmoded. Events far to the south, in mainland Scotland, have been evoked as the reason for this, but the connection is far from clear. Some of Shetland's brochs were partially demolished, and some were modified by the insertion of stone fittings in place of wooden ones, to convert the broch from a refuge for many people to a single family dwelling. Good examples of these inserted walls can be seen at Mousa, Jarlshof and Clickimin, and unexcavated examples at Burland. The most recent broch to be excavated, at Upper Scalloway, appeared to have been abandoned very soon after it had been built, although whether because the threat disappeared or because it appeared too soon cannot be determined.

Most of the internal additions, and the free standing houses of the immediate post-broch phase at Jarlshof, are circular in plan, with a central area containing a hearth surrounded by a series of alcoves formed by masonry piers which project inwards from the wall of the house. The roofs of these structures were corbelled, at least around the outer part, and they probably had a central smoke-hole which could be covered in inclement weather. This is a house-plan not known before from Shetland, and has been termed a "wheelhouse", on the basis of its resemblance, as seen from above, to the hub, spokes and rim of a wheel. It has been suggested that these structures may be the stone equivalents of the wooden roundhouses of which traces have been found further south.

Now appearing almost subterranean, the wheelhouses at Jarlshof were free-standing buildings among the ruins of earlier habitations.

The pottery associated with the wheelhouse period at Jarlshof and Clickimin looks very like pottery of a similar period from Orkney, where wheelhouses have not yet been identified, although earlier stone round houses are known. Wheelhouses occur in the Hebrides, but there the pottery of this period is readily distinguished from that found in Shetland. While this confusing situation cannot be resolved with our present knowledge, it can generally be remarked that the period at the end of the use of the brochs in Shetland is one of widening contacts with other parts of Scotland, and perhaps with areas further afield. From the wheelhouse levels at the two sites come fragments of glass and pottery of Roman type, which are likely to be loot or souvenirs rather than trade goods, although we know that the Romans explored these waters in their galleys as part of their search for secure northern frontiers. Other objects of bronze and glass indicate contact with native groups in southern Scotland, but whether these widened horizons were a result of fresh immigration, as a result of conquest or otherwise, or merely arose with the relaxation of the inward-looking defensive attitudes of preceding generations, we cannot say. Once more, the facts of archaeology are not sufficient to explain the reality of prehistory.

The majority of post-broch houses in Shetland are much less elaborate than the wheelhouses, being lightly built variants of the traditional Shetland oval house. Excavations near Underhoull broch in Unst suggested that some of these houses may have been in use throughout the broch period. If this is the case, it would help to explain the rather uneven distribution of brochs.

While most artefacts of this period are uninspiring, with a continuation of older forms supplemented by a few more bronze items, the pottery is more interesting. In the early Iron Age, pottery is rather plain, having lost the decoration of the Bronze Age, and vessels are bucket-shaped and decidedly utilitarian. About the date of the early forts and brochs, this plain, steatite-gritted ware becomes more elaborate, with the production of vase-like vessels with out-

Most post-broch houses were simple: a ruined oval house at Burraland broch, on the mainland shore opposite Mousa.

turned rims. At the height of the broch period incised decoration reappears, and pots begin to bear applied bands of clay, twisted or finger-pinched. In addition, non-steatitic wares become more popular, with a red-brown appearance when fired, in contrast to the older greys and drab browns, and a new variety of steatite ware appears, a fine fabric with a glossy black exterior made by burnishing the surface of the vessel. Towards the end of the broch-using phase a very distinctive vessel appears, a globular jar with out-turned rim and a finger-impressed cordon, or clay band, around the neck. This is closely associated with the wheelhouses. But after the passage of little more than two centuries, Shetland pottery had returned to its pre-Iron Age state, with only the occasional out-turned rim as a reminder of its former variety.

Just what this diversification and subsequent simplification means is difficult to determine. One explanation could be the gradual immigration of small groups of settlers, each bringing fresh ideas which were integrated into the local pottery traditions. A more ambitious scheme calls for the emergence of a divided population, with different classes of ware for different levels of society. The mundane archaeologist finds a simpler answer, that we know of this variety of pottery because a far greater number of sites have been dug from Iron Age times than those of any other period. As a result we have more Iron Age pottery to study, and in all probability what we are seeing is a complete range of pots for a complete range of purposes: slick, shiny black ware for best, red-brown ware for table use and the coarser varieties for cooking and storage. Decoration would vary with taste and fashion, but this does not necessarily mean Shetland fashion alone, for it is hard to believe that the emergence of a glossy, black, pottery type in Shetland, not long after a similar ware appears in regions under Roman influence, is a complete coincidence.

After what was, by archaeological standards, a hectic period of social upheaval accompanied by unprecedented changes in building practices, Shetland by about 400 AD seems to have settled back into a quieter pattern of life, with the turbulent Iron Age largely forgotten. The clusters of people around broch sites gradually thinned, as families moved out into the countryside, now safe from imminent attack, and life slipped back into the daily round of ploughing, herding and fishing. With this return to "normality" comes a lack of information from archaeology, and we move, by default rather than for a positive reason, into the Dark Ages.

VERY little is known about the end of the Iron Age in Shetland, and in many respects the way of life may have changed little from the later Iron Age until late Medieval times. However, it has become traditional to start a new archaeological period with the coming of Christianity to the north. In Shetland there is some support for change in this period in the appearance of a new type of habitation site and in the adoption of new artistic styles, the latter of the class generally called "Pictish". There is a lot of doubt about this. It is arguable that Christianity was brought to the islands by small groups of priest-monks around the end of the sixth century AD, and that these incomers found a population of older inhabitants in the islands, who for the sake of argument can be called Picts. It is also probable that, when they arrived in Shetland around 800 AD, as when they reached Orkney, Faroe and Iceland, pagan Norse settlers found colonies of clerics well established.

The native population, composed of the results of various influxes from Neolithic to late Iron Age times, seems to have been living a peaceful agricultural life during the fifth and sixth centuries AD, and the production of distinctive (some say all) pottery had ceased. Because of this, it is hard to locate their settlement sites, and it is quite likely that these may have disappeared below the homes of later Norse immigrants. There are a few Norse placenames which contain the element "petta", thought to signify Pictish links. These names, such as Pettaster, Pettadale or Pettifirth, are all in fairly remote and unattractive places, suggesting that, as the Norse settlers moved in, the last communities to become dominated by Norse culture may have been those living in the inland valleys.

It was formerly believed that a whole class of monument, the earth-houses or souterrains, could be attributed to the Picts. There are a few of these underground storeplaces in Shetland, all of them small by average Scottish standards, and mostly ruined. However, as recent excavations in mainland Scotland have shown that these structures were constructed as early as the beginning of the Iron Age, they must be ruled out as an indicator of the presence of the people we call the Picts, who only come into focus with the references to them in fourth and fifth century Roman writers. Shetland has produced, in excavations at Sandwick (Unst) (123) one of the very few Pictish period burials known in Scotland. A single skeleton was found below a low rectangular cairn made of quartz pebbles and edged with upright stone slabs. But apart from this site, other burials have proved as elusive as settlements. This leaves us only the remarkable sculptured stones, a series of metal objects worked in a similar artistic style and a handful of pebbles decorated with stained patterns of dots and circles, together with the evidence of placenames and rare literary documents, to support the idea of a people called the Picts.

"Pict" seems to have originated as a term for a confederation of northern tribes who fought against the Romans in

Shetland's sole dated Pictish burial was excavated at Sandwick, Unst.

Photo: G. Bigelow

mainland Scotland. It is probably a genuine name, rather than a Roman invention (despite the attractive Latin derivation from "pictus", painted), for the word was adopted by Scots in Ireland, Angles in Northumbria and the Norse when they arrived in Scotland. No written records of the Pictish language are known, apart from a number of largely indecipherable ogmic inscriptions on sculptured stones. It may well be that the Picts, if they had written language, only employed it on rare occasions, and kept records by memory or by the use of trained individuals, who would pass on traditions from generation to generation. This feature was found in the Irish peoples of this period, where the emergence of a fully written language is intimately associated with the arrival of Christianity.

Shetland possesses a small number of Pictish carved stones. These are slabs carved with various combinations of a standard set of subjects. Early examples bear abstract or animal motifs, and are usually incised upon rough boulders, while later examples often include human figures and Christian allusions, and are carved upon prepared flat slabs. There is much debate as to the function of the carved stones, which have been seen variously as grave-markers, memorials, boundary markers or gathering-points. However, there is no doubt that they were produced locally, as they are of local rock types, and thus represent at least one person working in the art style termed "Pictish".

There are very few examples of stones with supposedly early, non-Christian, motifs in Shetland, and until recently the only surviving example was the tiny Islesburgh eagle. Even this could be seen as having a religious link, for the eagle appears in later manuscripts as the symbol of St John the Evangelist. However, in 1992 an exceptionally fine stone was found in the graveyard at Mail, Cunningsburgh, showing a dog-headed man carrying an axe, a motif known from elsewhere in Scotland, notably Rhynie in Aberdeenshire. A lost slab from Cross Kirk, Esha Ness, is recorded as bearing only abstract symbols of the type usually dated to the earliest phase of Pictish stone-carving.

The recently-discovered Pictish carved stone from Mail, Cunningsburgh. *Photo: Val Turner*

The rest of Shetland's carved stones are of explicitly Christian type, including crosses or clerical figures in their design. A series of these stones has been recovered from the site of St Laurence's Church, Papil (West Burra) (119), while more have come from St Mary's, Cullingsburgh (Bressay) (121) and from St Ninian's Isle, off the west side of South Mainland (120). Some are of very high artistic quality, and most have found their way to the National Museum of Scotland in Edinburgh. Amongst the stones from Papil and St Ninian's Isle are fragments of stone altars or shrines, built from slabs held together at the corners by grooved posts of stone. One of the slabs from Papil has a view of a group of monks, in procession, with one mounted on a pony and the rest on foot. One of the walking monks carries a book satchel. Clearly, the priests of the Early Christian period in Shetland were not averse to the use of Pictish idioms in religious contexts. This, and the absence of any overtly Scottish/Irish remains, leads to the speculation that Shetland may have been converted by Pictish, rather than Scottish, clerics. There is also evidence for an eremitical monastic tradition in the church in Shetland, and this may be a result of Scottish influence.

The sites from which Pictish stones with Christian motifs have been recovered are all quite clearly the type of site where a church serving a local community might be located. That these communities were "Pictish" can hardly be doubted, and the treasure from St Ninian's Isle suggests that they may have been relatively wealthy, or at least may have included wealthy individuals. The treasure, found in excavations in 1958 on the site of a succession of churches overlying an Iron Age settlement, consists of a hoard of brooches, bowls and other items, all of silver and all skilfully worked with surface designs in the later Pictish mode. It is even possible they were made in Shetland, and, failing this, highly probable that they were made in northern Scotland. The treasure is now in the National Museum of Scotland in Edinburgh, with copies in Lerwick.

The small size of early Shetland churches might suggest a vertically divided population, with only the top stratum being converted to Christianity

The early Christian site at St Ninian's Isle looks over the superb sand tombolo to the Dunrossness hills.

The crowded burial ground at Papil, West Burra, lies over another pre-Norse Christian centre.

in the early days. If the Pictish element in the population was small but dominant, this would account for the obvious wealth of the early church and the Pictish art style, while allowing the churches to be small and widely scattered. Many of the early churches where surrounded by a circular earthen bank. The remains of such banks, which probably marked the area of sacred ground, can be seen at Papil, Cullingsburgh, St Ninian's Isle and Kirkaby (Unst). Evidence from Ireland suggests that important aspects of the liturgy took place in the open, with processions around the sacred enclosure, pausing at open-air shrines- a context for the "post-shrines" of which fragments have been found at St Ninian's Isle and Papil.

The presence of fragments of a type of polished stone, porfido verde antico, which derives originally from southern Greece, at St Ninian's Isle and Kebister, casts an interesting sidelight on the distant connections of early Christian Shetland. Even accepting that this stone, which was probably stripped from earlier decorative material in Rome and elsewhere, did not come direct from the quarry to Shetland, it indicates that the church in Shetland had access to at least small quantities of exotic imports. The recent discovery of similar fragments associated with the remains of the early church at Whithorn in Galloway opens up the intriguing possibility of an original Ninianic connection in the fifth, sixth or seventh century AD, rather than the late dedication assumed up until now by students of the Isle. This could mean that Shetland was brought very early into the mainstream of the developing church in Europe, rather than being part of the increasingly marginalised Celtic branch, and such a conclusion would be in line with evidence from Orkney and elsewhere.

In total contrast to the main churches, which seem to have been placed to serve local communities, are the second series of sites attributed to early Christians. These are a number of small clusters of dwellings built on the remotest and most inhospitable points of the coast. None are easy of access, and some are positively dangerous. There can be little doubt that these represent the dwellings of monastic communities on the lines of those found throughout northern Britain at this period, built far from other human settlement, in places which were calculated to provide a bare and austere existence, thus purifying the soul for its eventual passage heavenwards.

Because these sites are so remote, they have been little studied, but recent work has suggested that Shetland supported communities living in such locations for a considerable period of time, probably from pre-Norse days through the Viking period and into Norse-Medieval times. This can be inferred from the different shapes of foundation surviving. A number of sites have clusters of small, oblong foundations, arranged in rows. These resemble the small oval houses sometimes found on broch sites, and probably date to very late post-broch times. It is suspected that these buildings on promontories, in orderly array, mark the earliest of the eremitic communities.

A desolate retreat: Kame of Isbister.

A further group of sites, those on slightly better locations from an agricultural point of view, have rows of longhouse foundations, with slightly bowed walls. These cannot be other than Norse in origin, and can be equated with such Orcadian sites as Brough of Birsay and Deerness.

In some of the more remote establishments, such as those at Kame of Isbister (118) or Birrier of West Sandwick (117), on opposite sides of Yell Sound, life must have been very bare indeed, with little beyond seafowl and fish, perhaps supplemented by a few garden plots and some sheep on the hill behind. At the sites which appear to be Norse, the potential of the land is greater, as can be seen at sites like Bluemull (Unst) (116), Strandburgh (Fetlar) (125) and Kirk Holm near Sand (127). Here the buildings may have served partly as a

Facing Kame of Isbister across Yell Sound is Birrier of West Sandwick.

farm, with a monastic tradition more in keeping with recent times, emphasising austere self-sufficiency rather than penitential self-denial. The Norse appear to have taken some sites from earlier clerics, as attested by the fact that the centre of early Norse power was Papa Stour, a name which means "big island of the priests". A number of other "papa" placenames suggest the Norse discovery of clerical communities in residence.

There are doubtless eremitical sites yet to be discovered, on seaward-sloping promontories or offshore stacks. Such sites may be recognised by the orderly layout of the foundations, and the earlier sites are typified by very small buildings, little more than three metres by two metres internally at some sites. In a few cases, earlier fortifications seem to have been re-used, for example at Garth Ness. The houses on sites attributed to Norse clerics are larger, and of characteristic rectilinear plan. The key to identifying these sites is the absurdity of their location in practical terms. Not content with the permanent exposure of communal sites such as Strandburgh, the monks also built small cells in even more remote places, to allow members of the community to escape into total isolation.

Only the placename survives to tell of an early ecclesiastical establishment at Papil, Fetlar.

The ruins of such hermitages may be seen on the Clett, a precipitous stack north of Fetlar, and on such forbidding rocks as Freya Stack, off Foula.

In later times, small houses were constructed in out of the way places to house lepers. There is some doubt if these were sufferers from true leprosy or from a skin condition closely similar to leprosy, and perhaps derived from an unbalanced diet rich in salt fish. However, these unfortunates were shut out of society and made to live apart. But leper-houses were usually easily accessible by land, for donations of food were provided by the families of the afflicted. Also, Shetland traditions are long-lived and reliable, and many leper-house sites are pointed out to this day, while there are no traditions of such use for most of the truely remote settlements. So it seems safe to conclude that many stack and promontory sites are, indeed, early Christian hermitages.

At Ness of Garth, Sandness, a promontory fort found a new life as a monastic settlement.

Both strands of Christian tradition seem to have survived the Norse immigration, with church sites carrying on to form the locations of Medieval chapels, while the monastic practices of

Footings of a small sub-rectangular house at Ness of Garth.

earlier times were eventually translated into a Norse equivalent, and this despite the fact that for a century and a half the Norse settlers were nominally pagan.

To return to Pictish times, we have seen that there is a some evidence for the early church, and a series of tantalising glimpses of the Pictish traditions of at least part of the populace. But of the domestic structures of this period, not a trace has been recovered and firmly dated, except at Jarlshof, where the houses assigned to the late Pictish period were flimsily built and poorly preserved, and also possibly at Underhoull in Unst, where houses below a Norse house apparently began in use in the broch period but continued for many years thereafter.

It may be that the Picts chose locations which were the same as those favoured by incoming Norsemen in later years, so that Pictish settlement disappeared below Norse farms, while these in turn were obscured by generations of later crofts. Alternatively, houses may have been built of perishable materials, such as turf and wood, which have since decayed to leave no visible remains. This need not necessarily imply poverty. An all-timber house in a largely treeless environment would have been a potent symbol of

Possibly Pictish: a small oval house lying high in the rubble at Southpunds broch.

wealth. The uncertain examples at Jarlshof and Underhoull remain the only Pictish houses in Shetland. The problem for the archaeologist is that the Picts, if we may so call them, do not appear to have had any distinctive everyday artefacts, with the possible exception of rare painted pebbles. Thus even if house-sites of the correct date are found, these might not be recognised for what they were. Recently, excavations at Upper Scalloway have produced just such pebbles from a very late post-broch context, but otherwise little was learned about the character of the small houses, almost huts, associated with these finds.

Only church sites have produced specifically Pictish material, and even here we cannot be sure whether the priests, or a part of their flock, or the whole of the community, belonged to the greater Pictish culture. The Picts are a fine example of the way in which prehistorians can take a few attributes and use them to construct a "culture" which may have had no real basis in society. The only certain things about the Shetland Picts are that the Norse found people in Shetland they called "Picts" and that there a few objects in the art-style we call "Pictish". We cannot even prove that the two went together!

We have come, in terms of information, almost full circle, from the very earliest settlers, whose homes we have not discovered, to the Picts, about whom we know perhaps even less. But at every period we have seen how the distinctive character of Shetland has called forth responses from its inhabitants, forcing them to modify their lifestyles in tune with wind and weather, and to adapt to use all of the resources available to them. It therefore comes as something of a surprise to discover Shetland suddenly becoming, at the end of the eighth century AD, a "promised land" for large numbers of settlers.

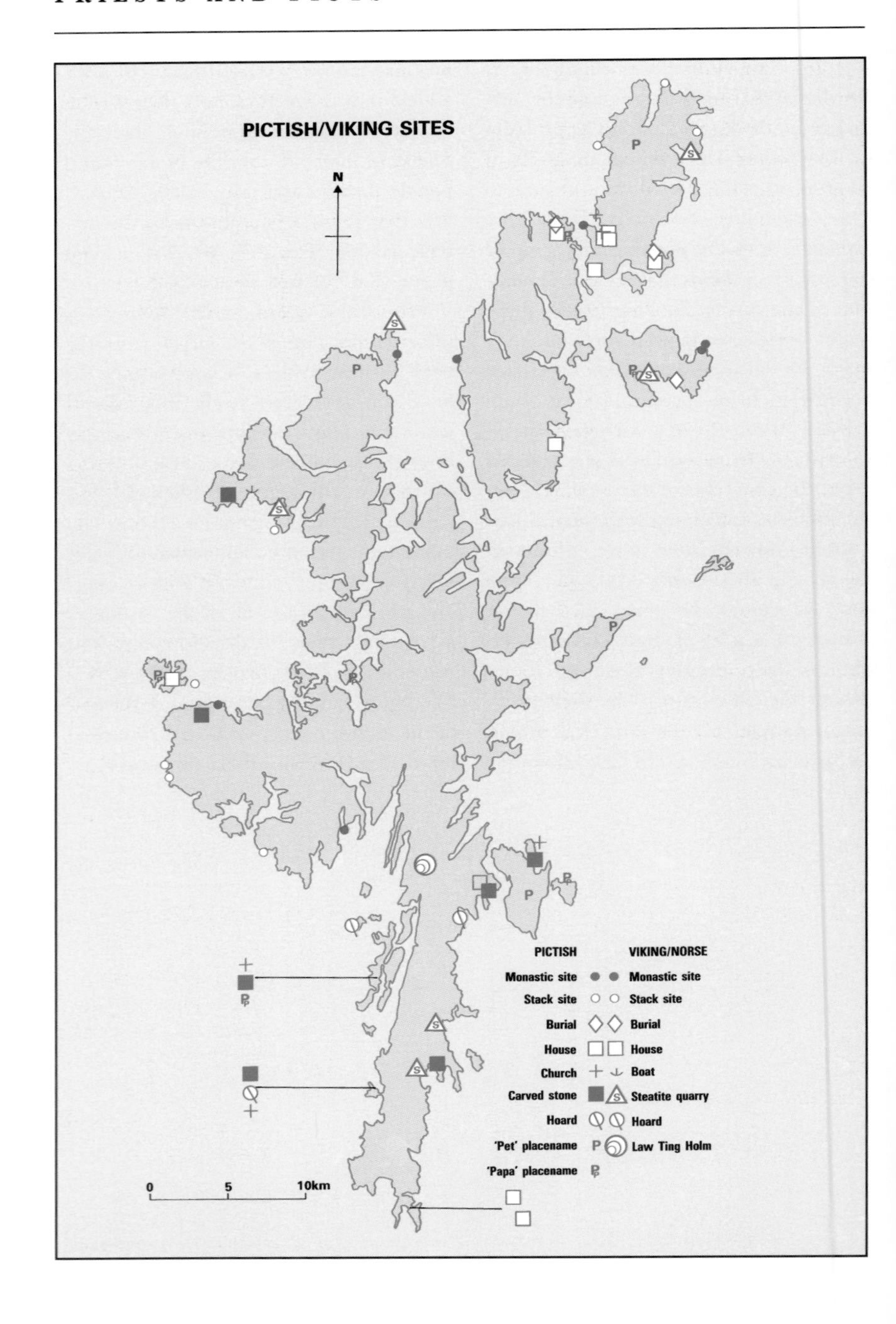
PICTISH/VIKING SITES
N
P
P
P
P
0
5
10km
PICTISH
VIKING/NORSE
Monastic site
Monastic site
Stack site
Stack site
Burial
Burial
House
House
Church
Boat
Carved stone
Steatite quarry
Hoard
Hoard
'Pet' placename
Law Ting Holm
'Papa' placename

WE know considerably more about the first Norse settlers than we do about their precursors in Shetland. They came from western and southern Norway, late in the eighth or early in the ninth century AD. Although the reason for earlier Viking raids all round the coasts of Britain was to plunder, it seems that the raiders kept their eyes open for likely territory to settle, and by Norwegian standards Shetland was an attractive and somewhat familiar landscape. Around 800 AD there appears to have been a critical economic situation in Norway: possibly a collapse of the farming system due to successive poor harvests. Ever-increasing numbers of Norsemen chose to cross to Shetland, bringing their families, goods and gear with them.

Compared with overcrowded Norway, Shetland seems to have been relatively empty at this time. There are no surviving legends or accounts of conquest in the later saga literature, but since this does not survive complete, this may not prove much. Just when the first settlement happened, and where, is a question unlikely ever to be answered. Unst or Fetlar might be a candidate, for local tradition maintains that a distinct race, neither Picts nor Norsemen, inhabited north-east Unst and eastern Fetlar. They were called Finns, or Finn-Men. These could perhaps be the first Scandinavians in Shetland, for "Finn" could derive from the word for white, or fair - "fionn" in Scots Gaelic or "wen" in the older British form of the Celtic tongue - "f" for "w" is a well-known north-east Scottish pronunciation even nowadays. Placenames with the element "Finn" survive in Unst, Fetlar and Nesting.

We know from the way in which the names of places are constructed (and over 99 percent of Shetland names have Norse derivations), and the personal names within these placenames, that the bulk of the more important settlers came from the area around, and south of, present day Trondheim, which was later for centuries to be the seat of the bishopric covering Shetland. From the elements of some placenames we can attempt to analyse the settlement process. It has been suggested that names ending in "by" or "sta/ster" (Melby, Norby, Bousta, Elvister) were early farms, with "bister" farms following (such as Symbister, Wadbister) then "setter" farms last of all (Dalsetter, for example). However, the real situation would have been much more complex, and just as today names may have been changed over time, and some would have been imported ready-formed from the ancestral home in Norway.

It is assumed, because few non-Norse, or pre-Norse, names survive - perhaps only the island names, Unst, Yell and Fetlar - that Norse linguistic culture swamped whatever "native" elements remained, and we must assume that this represents a real, political, takeover of power. "Shetland" itself is a Norse name, Hjaltaland, probably meaning "the hilt land". It is not known how many natives there were to be taken over, and it has even been suggested that Shetland had been largely depopulated by some undefined agency, perhaps a plague, before the Viking settlement. Unlike neighbouring Orkney, there is little to suggest continuity between the Pictish and the Norse periods, but the evidence for this period is, in any case, extremely scanty. Although we have information deduced by inference from Scandinavia and elsewhere, for the specific early references to Shetland are few, there is little to show in the way of physical remains. Only at Jarlshof is a sequence of buildings from the early Norse settlement onwards clearly visible. Buildings of a somewhat later date have been revealed by excavation at Underhoull (122) and Sandwick (Unst) (123) and da Biggins (Papa Stour). The two first sites are still visible, although ruinous. Other buildings, possibly of early Norse date, can be discerned at a few unexcavated sites, notably Belmont (Unst), Gossabrough (Yell) (124) and Catpund (South Mainland). The promontory sites discussed in the last chapter seem to include some Norse ones.

There are a small number of other sites which may be of Viking date: possible boat burials at Wick of Aith (Fetlar) (126) and Breakon (Yell) (33). Doubtless many standing stones are of Norse date, erected as sailing marks.

Much modified, the original Viking house at Jarlshof ended its life as a cow-byre.

True Viking-period houses are rare: this example of a Norse-Medieval period house at Sandwick, Unst, dates from the late thirteenth or early fourteenth century, well after the Viking period.

Apart from the material from excavated sites, early Norse objects are remarkably scarce, with a few splendid exceptions such as the brooches from Oxna and Gulberwick. Some sand-dune sites regularly produce small items, such as fragments of composite bone combs or blue glass beads, but even so there is really very little evidence compared with, say, the Neolithic, even allowing for the shorter duration of the Norse period.

With the coming together of archaeology and early history (and Shetland is quite well-endowed with documentary material compared with most of Scotland) more complicated questions can be asked, such as where on Papa Stour was the farm owned by Duke Hakon in 1299. But for the present purpose it is enough to restrict discussion to three simple questions: what were the physical structures built by the early Norse settlers; where do these survive to be seen, and why are there not more of them.

Although Pictish sub-rectangular buildings, most likely cattle-byres, may already have existed, the Norse settlers certainly deserve the credit for transforming Shetland house-plans from curvilinear to rectilinear, although in fact some of their earlier houses had bowed, rather than straight, long walls. So far as the evidence from Jarlshof goes, Norse houses began as large, but relatively simple, halls, apparently designed for a largely communal life, and gradually developed towards greater subdivision, with extra units being added to the end or side of existing houses as need, status or fashion changed. Individual houses were rebuilt or modified repeatedly. The earliest Norse dwelling at Jarlshof was in use for two centuries, by the end of which time it had been changed radically from the original. This pattern of large,relatively undivided, early houses giving way to greater subdivision is echoed in Iceland and Greenland, although the settlements there were three and four generations later, respectively, than in Shetland.

By around 1000 AD, at which date it is customary to end the Viking Age in favour of the Norse or Norse-Medieval period, houses in Shetland varied considerably in plan. The larger ones had stone walls (except, on parallels from elsewhere in the Norse Atlantic settlements, that one gable may have been of wood), and had thatched gable-ended roofs supported by rows of posts running down the centre of the floor. Smaller examples were of stone or (probably, for none survive) of turf or even wood, with roofs supported on the wall-heads alone. In the larger houses long, kerbed, central hearths were flanked by raised benches used both for eating and sleeping: as in earlier periods, except for severe weather Shetlanders lived out of doors much more than today. At one end of the dwelling a partitioned area formed the kitchen. Smaller houses

Probably dating from two hundred years or more after the Viking settlement, this combined house and byre at Jarlshof has the byre very sensibly at the downslope end.

probably combined all functions in a single room.

Outhouses proliferated. Byres and barns, some with corn-drying kilns, have been found at Jarlshof, although the excavator's identification of a "bath-house" may, for some, seem to stretch the evidence a little. At Sandwick (Unst), excavation revealed a byre doorway which solved a long standing problem: the foundation plans of "byres" at Jarlshof had entrances too narrow to allow fully grown cattle, even diminutive ones, to enter or leave. At Sandwick the entrance survived to a metre high, and was very clearly cow-shaped - it broadened as it rose until, at waist-height, it was just wide enough to allow cattle to pass through.

Many artefacts have been found in excavation: stone pots and net sinkers, hones for metal tools, bone needles and pins abound. Bone combs and glass beads, as well as a few small slate graffiti, perhaps rough drafts of designs to be executed on stone or wood, suggest a less utilitarian side to life, as do the tiny model rotary querns from a few sites, which can only be toys. When found away from excavations, many of the more mundane objects are hard to identify positively as Viking or early

Later still are the foundations of this small barn, with what is probably the base of a corn-drying kiln at the far side.

Norse rather than Medieval or even later: only rare examples, fine metalwork, delicately worked bone pins and a few distinctive hones are easily recognised as of Viking date.

When the first settlers arrived from what is now Norway, they were predominantly pagan, and pagan burials have been found. Characteristic of such burials are bronze "tortoise" brooches, which usually occur in pairs. Other stray finds, like the Oxna and Gulberwick brooches, may also be from unrecognised, and now destroyed, burials. There is little to suggest that such fine objects were made locally. It is quite possible that there are undiscovered pagan graves, for there has been no systematic search. Characteristically these graves are oval, or pointed-oval in plan, and from four to six metres long, formed of low mounds of small stones and kerbed by larger stones, often set upright. Disappointingly for archaeologists, the new population was progressively converted to Christianity not long after they arrived, and deposition of grave goods became increasingly rare.

Interestingly, in view of the usual picture of Viking predispositions, there seems to have been a degree of toleration

At Breakon, Yell, what may be a boat-shaped Viking grave lies beside earlier cairns in an area of deep sand-dunes.

for the established Christian sites, and placenames with ''papa'' elements suggest that Christian communities not only existed at the Viking settlement but continued in existence. The pagan Norse religion was not an evangelistic one, and it is easy to picture the Viking settler shaking his head in wonderment over the ''crazy Christians'' living on promontories and stacks. On the other hand, some of the Norse settlers were either Christian, or adopted Christianity long before the ''official'' conversion of Shetland and Orkney, when Earl Sigurd was baptised by Olaf Trigvesson in AD 995. It is known that some of the settlers of Iceland were Christian and had come to Iceland from Norse settlements in the northern and western isles of Scotland before that date, and indeed it may be that by the time of the coversion of their leader the majority of the population was already Christian, although doubtless pagan elements lingered on, in the form of superstitions.

Once Christianity was formally recognised as the official religion, many former ecclesiastical sites may have been brought back into use, while those with continuity of use were probably remodelled. Various remote locations such as Strandburgh (Fetlar) and Kirk Holm

Kirk Holm, between Reawick and Sand, may have housed a Christian Norse monastic community: traces of rectangular houses lie at the north end of the island (left side of the photograph).

The bed of the Catpund Burn at Cunningsburgh displays the hollows left by the extraction of steatite bowls.

This excavated section of bedrock is completely covered with Medieval quarrying scars: much of the valley at Catpund Burn is probably similarly scarred under the thin turf.

(West Mainland) seem to have monastic establishments with Norse-style house foundations, as already mentioned. No evidence for early Norse churches comparable for that from Orkney has so far been discovered, although tradition points out the site of churches of 11th or 12th century type, with round towers, at Papil and Tingwall. The chapel ruins at St Ninian's Isle, although not likely to be earlier than the late 12th century, overlie an earlier structure, probably ecclesiastical, and it has even been suggested that the treasure found there was hidden in a church because a church was less likely to be attacked by raiders than a secular building, putting an altogether different gloss on the quasi-historical records of Viking raiders.

The Norse settlers seem to have expanded the use of soapstone, although it was known and used before. They worked the main outcrops in Cunningsburgh and also smaller deposits at Hillswick, Fethaland, Houbie (96) and elsewhere. On more remote outcrops traces of Viking-period working can still be seen, but at more accessible areas, such as Catpund Burn at Cunningsburgh, later quarrying has largely removed early forms, at least on exposed surfaces. Chisel marks and the cores of bowls can be seen, as can large heaps of "wasters" (fragments broken in manufacture) and chippings. This easily worked material, with which the settlers were familiar from their homeland, was an important resource for making vessels, loom weights and net sinkers, spindle-whorls and even jewellery — pendants and armlets are known. Shetland steatite probably makes up the bulk of such material found throughout the Norse settlement areas in Britain and Ireland. Is it merely coincidence that near to the main outcrop is Cunningsburgh — "the King's fort"?

But where are all the houses of the Viking settlers? Only a handful of settlement sites are known, while we can list well over a hundred sites from the Iron Age. The answer is twofold. First, except where defence is a consideration, the ordinary houses of any period are often relatively slight structures, and it may be that wood or turf was used as a building material. But second, and more important, is the fact that many modern crofts bear Norse names, and occupy sites which fulfil the ideal for Norse settlement: above the farmland, overlooking the bay and with easy access to the hill grazing lands: it seems that the Norse farms lie below their later Medieval successors; an idea recently proved for one site by excavation at da Biggins in Papa Stour.

Many modern Shetlanders display an extreme attachement to their "Viking ancestry", and this can cause problems for the student of anthropology or history, for historical, genetic and anatomical evidence suggests a very mixed ancestry with the Norse element not preponderant. But at least for their homes the Shetlanders can claim an unchallenged Norse pedigree: in shape, organisation and location the changes since the Viking settlement remained essentially minor until relatively recently, at least for those buildings which housed ordinary farming folk. At some stage in the Mediaeval period the so-called "Norse mill" was introduced into Shetland. This is a small mill, essentially a water-powered rotary quern with the upper stone turned by a direct drive from a horizontal paddle wheel, and very suitable for use on small streams. Until recent discoveries in Orkney, there was some doubt as to whether or not this type of mill (which was thought to be borrowed from Mediterranean examples) was actually an early Norse introduction. Now there is an excavated example in Orkney which is certainly of the Norse period, but to complicate matters recent excavations in Ireland have dated a very sophisticated horizontal mill, in this case tide-driven, to the pre-Norse period. It may well be that these mills were first discovered by Viking settlers in Ireland,

One legacy from Norse times is the practice of building boat shelters, noosts, above the high-tide mark. This example at Burra Ness in Yell has been repaired within the past few generations, but many noosts occupy traditional locations.

rather than in the Mediterranean, and spread wherever they went. Be that as it may, none of the countless ruined mills which line streams in Shetland can be dated earlier than the eighteenth century: such integral parts of the agricultural economy would have been regularly maintained and periodically rebuilt in situ, so that finding a Viking mill would

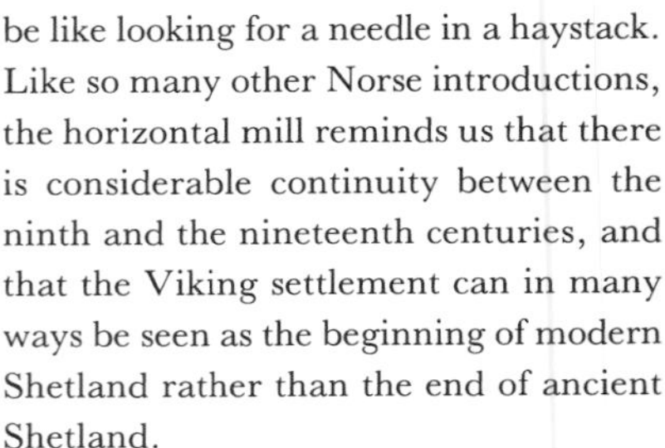

be like looking for a needle in a haystack. Like so many other Norse introductions, the horizontal mill reminds us that there is considerable continuity between the ninth and the nineteenth centuries, and that the Viking settlement can in many ways be seen as the beginning of modern Shetland rather than the end of ancient Shetland.

But the subject of "Norse" mills is one that draws us towards out conclusion. This survey of the remains of early Shetlanders has repeatedly thrown up instances of dating "by tradition" that have stood up to archaeological scrutiny. Shetland tradition recognises various "folk", who are associated with various types of ruin. The "trows" (trolls) or "peerie folk" are associated with various pre-Iron Age sites, such as the houses and fields at Trolligarts (West Mainland) (14) or the numerous burnt mounds or "trowie knowes". In every case, "trow" attributions appear to refer to pre-Iron Age sites. Next come the "Picts", and according to tradition they built the brochs, and forts, a few green mounds and the souterrains ("Pict's hooses"). Again, while not the Picts the art-historian knows, the attributed sites all appear to be of broadly Iron Age date. The mysterious "Finns" or "Finn-men" mentioned above, possibly pre-Norse and certainly contemporary with the "Picts" have few traditional attributions: the Funzie Girt, a great stone bank meandering across north and east Fetlar, is the only major monument, although such placenames as Finnister, in Nesting, may derive from the same source. Next

A typical "Norse" mill at Huxter, Sandness.

again come the Vikings, or Norsemen. Anything dating before the date of full recorded history, and particularly before the acquisition of Shetland by Scotland, is likely to be labelled ''Viking'' or ''Norse'', but interestingly the label is very rarely applied to pre-Norse remains. Last of all, and outwith the scope of this survey, are the ''Dutchmen'', Hanseatic traders and Low Countries fishermen who receive the credit for miscellaneous mounds and buildings near the shore, usually as ''Hollanders Knowe'' or ''Dutchmen's Graves''.

So far as archaeologists can test Shetland tradition, it is both consistent from district to district and accurate in broad terms. If there are going to be major advances in our understanding of the ways of Shetland's early inhabitants, it may be that archaeologists should stop showing surprise when local traditions are vindicated and start using those traditions to guide research. Who better to understand the prehistory of Shetland than a crofter living in a house on a thousand-year-old site and farming in a style essentially unchanged for even longer. In Shetland, more than most places perhaps, prehistory, history and tradition are woven together in a way which can allow valid inferences about the past.

So as visitors view the archaeological remains discussed here, let them remember that these are the vestiges of real people, individuals whose works have been preserved by the random hand of fate. And look around at the green fields and remember how the soil of each green acre was won painstakingly from barren moorland. The past is very close to the surface in Shetland, and in Shetlanders. As a local antiquarian put it, ''in short, there must have taken place the same constant warfare against cold and hunger that has ever gone on in Shetland''.

Life in Shetland has never been easy: deserted crofthouse and fields at Gruting.

GAZETTEER

THIS is a selective list of archaeological remains. It includes the best examples of all classes, but is not comprehensive, in that some good sites are omitted because they are very hard to find, while a few sites have been included because they have fine settings, although the visible remains may not be exceptionally good. The best-preserved sites are marked by an asterisk, and these would serve the person on a flying visit, or those with only a passing interest in prehistory.

The list is arranged by period and within period by area: Unst, Yell, Fetlar, Whalsay, Mainland (N to S), Bressay, Fair Isle. Smaller islands are dealt with in the sections for the adjacent land area. Each site has its reference on the National Grid, and visitors would be well advised to obtain the four sheets of the 1:50000 Ordnance Survey map for Shetland for guidance as well as for the many additional monuments marked upon them. The map sheet numbers are given before the Grid Reference for each site. Most of the sites described here are marked on these sheets.

The inclusion of a site does not guarantee any right of access. A few of the sites (Jarlshof, Clickimin, Ness of Burgi, Stanydale) are cared for by Historic Scotland on behalf of the nation, and at the first two access is permitted at set times only.

Only Jarlshof has an admission charge. Most of the other sites are on open land and accessible to any visitor who takes care not to damage walls or fences, shuts gates, keeps dogs on the leash and generally behaves responsibly. When in doubt about access, always ask: the author has never been refused access to a Shetland site without a good reason, and thanks the hospitable Shetlanders accordingly.

One last word: these structures have stood for up to four thousand years. They represent the legacy of past generations who have left no other record of their passing. Archaeological sites are precious remnants, part of our national heritage. Visitors should not scramble over crumbling walls, or try their hands at a little rebuilding, but leave the monuments as they find them, so that future generations will be able to enjoy the pleasure of searching out, for themselves, the traces of their earliest ancestry. Most of the sites listed, too, are scheduled ancient monuments, and it is a criminal offence to damage or disturb them, or to use a metal detector.

In visiting Shetland sites, it is as well to remember that they may be some distance from roads, and in uninhabited barren country with few passers-by. Be well-clothed: Shetland's weather can change swiftly. If you are going any distance from the roads, take a map and compass and be able to use them.

Good visiting. Once the sites in this list have been exhausted, there are many more on the Ordnance Survey maps worth examining, and there is always the possibility of discovering new remains, even in more settled parts, once the observer knows what to seek.

Typical sub-peat walling of Neolithic or Bronze Age date at Scord of Wadbister.

1 ***Funzie Girt, Fetlar, boundary dyke**
1 HU617931-HU626945

A long stretch of remarkably massive tumbled drystone walling, running across the shoulder of a moorland hill. This is probably the finest prehistoric boundary dyke in Shetland. (Due north from airstrip, past Hjaltadans (37), over the saddle between Stackaberg and Vord Hill. The dyke runs from the saddle N, then NW, around the side of the hill, ending near the impressive cliffs at East Neep. On RSPB Reserve, check first with warden.)

2 ***Benie Hoose, Whalsay, house**
2 HU586653

This fine example of a clover-leaf plan house, close to a second (3), was excavated by Charles Calder, the excavator of Stanydale (18). Despite the presence of a number of cairns of possible heel-shaped plan in the vicinity, there is no reason to suppose that either house was anything other than a typical farmhouse. (Above the shore, 1km NE of Isbister: in dry weather the approach over the hill from the W is a pleasant walk.)

3 ***Stones of Yoxie, Whalsay, house**
2 HU587653

Just downslope from the Benie Hoose (2), this too is an excavated example of a simple prehistoric house. The "forecourt" of the "temple", as interpreted by the excavator, is probably no more than a porch or windbreak protecting the entrance. (As for Benie Hoose.)

4 **Loch of Sandwick, Whalsay, houses & fields** 2 HU536618
Remains of at least four prehistoric houses of varied plan, together with two burnt mounds and several stretches of field walling occupy an extensive area on the northern shore of Sand Wick. (300 to 600m W of road, down hill from Sandwick crofts.)

5 **Beorgs of Uyea, North Roe, axe quarry** 2 HU327900
A large outcrop of felsite has been quarried to produce a hollow, which has been roofed. The felsite was used for the production of polished stone knives and axes, and the litter from the roughing-out of these tools lies all around the quarry pit. It includes semi-finished rough-outs, abandoned before final polishing began. This is the most easily found of a number of working floors spread across the nearby slopes, where this favoured rock-type outcrops in many places. (A track runs W from North Roe School for 3km, until it swings NE. The route to the site is along S shore of the Mill Loch beyond this change in direction. A tall, modern, cairn lies on the skyline, and the site is reached just before this. A rough walk, across unfrequented moorland.)

6 **Black Water, Eshaness, house** 3 HU229786
A ruinous oval house of rather small dimensions. (Immediately to the N of the B9078 road, 300m beyond the turnoff for Leascole.)

7 **Grevasand, Hillswick, house** 3 HU274762
An oval house, with many traces of field boundaries and cairns. (On a dip in the ridge on the W side of Hillswick peninsula, just under 1km SW of the road end.)

8 **Punds Water, Mangaster, house and walls** 3 HU323714
A massively built house, with an associated field system apparently bounded by a stout wall which closes the neck of a promontory just beyond the house. (750m NW from parking place on road just E of Mangaster, over a small hill, to the chambered cairn (44), then a further 500m around the S shore of Punds Water.)

9 ***Bays Water, Mavis Grind, houses & fields** 3 HU335675
A well-preserved field system, incorporating four houses, one of which, an oval 11m by 9, is apparently of a similar plan to the main house at Gruting School (19). There are many clearance cairns, and a number of "rude stone implements", mainly stone plough tips, have been found in this area. (N end of Bays Water, 1km NW of Busta.)

10 **Lunning, Lunnasting, house** 3 HU510671
A well-preserved prehistoric house, standing up to 1m high. The structure is 10m in diameter, with a thick wall surrounding an interior which has traces of four alcoves. The

entrance was on the south side, where there is an annexe, or a small yard. To the NE is a small field or yard, and to the east E field walling is visible. (150m S of trig point on Lunning Head.)

11 **Longa Ness, Noonsbrough, houses** 3 HU288579

Two prehistoric houses lie in a low valley between Longa Ness and Noonsbrough, with a series of fields walls and clearance cairns around them. One of the houses lies directly below a sheep shelter, the second being about 100m to the E. A ruined cairn lies on a hillside ledge overlooking the settlement area from the E. (From road end at Noonsbrough, walk along track past farm and then NW across hilltop and down to site, about 1km each way.)

12 ***Newing, South Nesting, houses & fields** 3 HU467559-HU477567

A remarkable series of prehistoric houses and enclosures, together with clearance cairns and walls, beside the North Nesting road. A small house in a field system lies 200m W of the deserted croft at South Newing (HU 467558), and another immediately E of the road 100m E of the croft (HU 470559), has a windbreak outside its entrance. 500m along the road, beyond North Newing, and at the foot of the road embankment, is a third example (HU 474565). This is roughly circular, with numerous field walls nearby. 170m further, and near the E side of the road, is an oval house 8m by 7, with its entrance on the SE and an enclosure attached to its SW side. The final example (HU 477567) immediately beside the road on the E, lies 120m beyond, and is 8m by 6, again with an entrance on the SE side. (Along the B9075 road from South Nesting to Bretabister.)

13 **Finnister, houses and fields** 3 HU462517

Two oval houses lie on the hillside, near to a perennial spring, with a splendid view across the Isles of Gletness. (On a shoulder of the hill, SW of the deserted croft and at about the same height on the hillside.)

14 **Trolligarts, Sandness Road, houses & fields** 3 HU245524

Two oval houses (at least) and a complex scatter of field walls and clearance cairns lie around and below a group of later croft buildings, sheep pens and cabbage patches. Two chambered cairns lie nearby. This site has never been properly surveyed, and is potentially as extensive and interesting as any in West Mainland Shetland. (250m NE of the A971 Sandness road at a stream flowing into W end of Loch of Flatpunds. Note that the site is well to the S of the placename on the 1:50000 OS map.)

15 ***Scord of Brouster, Walls, houses & fields** 3 HU255516

16 **Pinhoulland, Walls, houses & fields** 3 HU259497

17 **Loch of Grunnavoe, Walls, houses** 3 HU258494

These locations are the nuclei of a belt of early settlement remains running down the W side of the Voe of Browland. Brouster, recently excavated, has four houses, a possible square, kerbed, burial cairn, a system of interlinked field walls and over 100 clearance cairns. Pinhoulland has as many as seven houses, a few short traces of walls and many cairns. Grunnavoe has three houses and many cairns. Between these are numerous scattered cairns and stretches of walling, often partly submerged by the peat. Associated with this assemblage of agricultural remains are a number of cairns, some of them chambered (see 59). The main house at Brouster has massive orthostats dividing the side alcoves, and dates to before 2000BC, when it replaced an earlier wooden structure. Some of the cairns, which look small, have sub-peat basal diameters of over 2m. There is good evidence from this site that soils in the area were much richer during the settlement phase. Published excavation report on Scord of Brouster. (Brouster lies to the N of the junction at Bridge of Walls, and the remains run S along the voe and over to Loch of Grunnavoe 2km away)

18 ***Stanydale, "temple" & houses** 3 HU285502

The best known, although by no means the most extensive, of the prehistoric settlement areas in West Mainland Shetland, Stanydale is remarkable for the main site, which is a double-sized version of the oval transepted house. Three rather ruined oval houses of normal size lie near to the main building, while a fourth, which is in a clearer state, lies on the approach track. Numerous fragments of walling lie around the area, with a large number of grass-grown clearance cairns. A setting of upright stones curves round the south side of the main building, but is not of any distinct form, being neither stone alignment nor stone circle. A number of cairns lie on hilltops to both north and south. The main building has two post-holes in the centre, and may have been roofed, a formidable undertaking in wood-scarce Shetland. Its entrance is from the centre of a curved facade like that of the heel-shaped cairns, and the size and plan of the structure led the excavator to suggest that the building was a temple. It must certainly have been an edifice of some importance, and presumably some sort of gathering place, whether religious or secular. The well-preserved house, which has been excavated, shows a variant on the usual plan, with a main oval chamber from which a small circular compartment runs off at the inner end. The entrance has been provided with a porch, or windbreak, curving around the doorway, which could otherwise have been exposed to the SW. Pottery from this house and the "temple" suggest a long life, from the late Neolithic right through the Bronze Age. Guardianship monument, always open. See also Historic

Scotland guidebook. (Signposted and route marked by posts across moor, from road to Gruting, 1km S of the turn for Stanydale farm. Do not take the road to the farm.)

19 **Gruting School, houses**
3 HU282499
A large oval house lying north of the head of Gruting Voe is the best preserved member of a group of three houses. One of the others is bisected by the road, while the second lies below a small garage beside the road. The main house is a large oval, and was not transepted. (N of the road, just above the former Gruting School.)

20 **Ness of Gruting, houses & fields**
3 HU276483-HU283482
Two groups of remains lie close together. Two houses and a burnt mound lie on the SW ridge of the hill. Further to the E is a single house. Both groups lie within enclosures, and the hillside is divided up into a series of small fields, some of which appear to be terraced into the slope. (The easiest approach is along the ridge from the highest point on the road between Seli Voe and Scutta Voe, approximately 1km. The site lies halfway down the slope to the shore.)

21 **Jamie Cheyne's Loch, Scalloway, house** 4 HU398428
A well-preserved house of oval form, showing internal sub-divisions, and with two large enclosures attached. The surrounding slopes are dotted with cairns and fragments of walling, the remains of an extensive field system. (100 m S of the loch, on a moorland ridge.)

22 ***Clickimin, Lerwick, house**
4 HU464408
A small, well-rebuilt, oval house of clover-leaf plan represents the first phase of a long use of the site, and may have had other, less substantial, buildings around it. (See below for Iron Age elements.) Guardianship monument, no charge. See also Historic Scotland guidebook. (Signposted, to right of A970 road leaving Lerwick for S.)

23 **Punds Geo, Uppersound, house**
4 HU458392
A ruined house, 10m by 7, lies on a small terrace. The entrance seem to be on the W side. Another, more ruined structure, lies 100m to the N, and may also be a house. (W side of Voe of Sound at Punds Geo, 1km S of the head of the voe.)

24 **Ux Ness, West Burra, house & field**
4 HU383357
A small, oval house with large blocks forming the partitions between the internal alcoves. A boundary wall encloses the house and a number of clearance cairns. (Immediately beyond the end of the bridge from Trondra, above the road.)

25 **Dalsetter, Boddam, houses & fields**
4 HU403157
Three oval houses lie within a fragmentary enclosure wall built of large blocks. Within the main enclosure are traces of slighter walls, and a number of clearance cairns

testify to early agriculture. The houses are of medium size, from 10m to 12 in overall length. (To right of road from Boddam to Troswick, on S-facing slope.)

26 ***Jarlshof, Sumburgh, houses** 4 HU399096

The earliest remains visible at this, the most complex excavated site in Shetland, comprise a cluster of smallish oval houses, which show the characteristic "clover-leaf" internal plan. These were replaced towards the end of the Bronze Age by a group of roughly circular houses, of similar size. A number of querns, used for grinding grain, have been left in situ, and more artefacts can be seen in the visitor centre. (See below for Iron Age and later remains.) Guardianship monument, limited opening hours, entrance charge. See also Historic Scotland guidebook. (Signposted, parking at Sumburgh Hotel.)

GAZETTEER: Neolithic/Bronze Age — ritual and funerary

27 **Muckle Heog, Unst, cairns** 1 HP630108, HP631107

On the summit of the hill are the remains of a large cairn which was excavated last century and produced bones and steatite pottery. Not far to the NW is a heel-shaped cairn with traces of the facade showing, and the remains of two cists, but no trace of a chamber. (Summit of hill, 700m NNW from entrance to Hagdale)

A massive pile of stone marks a ruined burial cairn at Punds Water.

28 **Rounds of Tivla, Unst, cremation cemetery** 1 HP616107

Downhill from a group of three round cairns, one containing a cist, lies this group of three circular earthworks. Only one retains its earlier recorded form, and this consists of three low concentric banks, with two shallow ditches between, surrounding a central stony spread some 9m in diameter. The ruined sites nearby were apparently of similar character. This may be a Bronze Age burial monument of a type related to the enclosed cremation cemeteries of more southern parts. (1km NE of Gue, Baltasound, near the top of Crussa Field.)

29 **Hill of Caldback, Unst, chambered cairn** 1 HP607067

Two heel-shaped cairns stand on this

hill. The one on the summit is badly delapidated, but measures about 16m across, with a facade on the eastern side. There are no clear signs of cist or chamber. The lower cairn, at the foot of the slope on the west side of the hill, is better preserved, and of similar dimensions. The facade is framed by two orthostats, and the cairn is unusual in having three cists, but no entrance passage and chamber. This is the only definite example of the combination of heel-shaped cairn and cists. (The hill is W of the highest point on the A968 Baltasound-Uyeasound road.)

30 **Watlee, Unst, chambered cairn**
1 HP596051

A smaller cairn, 10m in diameter, with vague traces of a central chamber. A small oval foundation on the north side is later. (The cairn lies immediately W of the main A968 road, overlooking Loch of Watlee.)

31 ***Bordastubble, Burragarth, Unst, stone** 1 HP578034

Possibly the most massive of the Shetland standing stones, this example is of gneiss, stands 3.8m high and is up to 2.7m thick. Traces of packing stones can be seen at the foot of the stone, but it is not certain that these are original, rather than a later attempt to prop up the block, which leans towards the south-west. (N of the road to Lund.)

32 **Clivocast, Unst, standing stones**
1 HP606007, HP604005

A narrow stone, 3m tall but only 0.9m wide at the base, stands on the slopes above Uyea Sound. A second, squatter, monolith stands downslope. A possible Viking grave was found many years ago near the latter stone. (S of the road to Muness, on the hill out of Uyeasound.)

33 **Breakon, Yell, cairns**
1 HP528053

A rather ruinous oval house is one of the features of this sand-dune area, which also has several substantial but rather featureless cairns and enclosures, as well as a possible Viking grave. (Follow track from Breakon Farm.)

34 **Gutcher, Yell, standing stone**
1 HU548985

A modest standing stone, of grey gneiss, overlooks the ferry crossing to Fetlar. (500m S of the ferry terminal, between the road to North Sandwick and the shore.)

35 **Lumbister, Yell, stone alignment**
1 HU487964

On an area of grass to the east of a ruined sheep pen is a linear setting of small boulders. These are arranged in three parallel lines running from NE to SW; each about 60m long and spaced about 15m apart. The central line is crossed by a short line of larger boulders, oriented N to S and more closely spaced. This is the best example in Shetland of a type of monument more common in Caithness. (On the S shore of Loch of Lumbister, reached up the valley from the road at Colvister.)

36 **Windhouse, Yell, chambered cairn**
1 HU487917

This heel-shaped cairn has been built on a steep slope, with the facade, built on very large blocks, facing W, downslope. The body of the cairn merges with the slope behind. There is a partly excavated broch by the large ruined house on the hilltop above. (N of the A968 road at the head of Whale Firth.)

37 **Hjaltadans, Stackaberg, Fetlar, circle** 1 HU618928

A ring of large blocks surrounds a flat area, within which is a low circular earthen bank. In the centre are two large blocks of stone, standing side by side. The date, period and function of this monument are unknown. (750m N of Fetlar airstrip. On RSPB Reserve, check first with warden.)

38 ***Ripple Stone, Fetlar, standing stone** 1 HU627905

A 2.3m tall block of schist, this is an unusually slender standing stone for Shetland, being only 1m by 0.4m at the base, and tapering above this. (Between the road and the sea at the E end of Feal.)

39 **Skaw Voe, Whalsay, standing stone** 2 HU589665

A large boulder, 1.5m high, stands 50m from the shore, and nearby are two fallen or broken stones which once stood upright. (Middle of bay, halfway between the road and the sea.)

40 ***Pettigarths Field, Yoxie, Whalsay, cairn** 2 HU585653

On the rise above the Benie Hoose (2) is a miniature heel-shaped cairn, reduced to its foundations. The cairn has a diameter of only 5m, and the chamber, which is polygonal, is 1m across. It has a narrow passage leading to it from the facade. A cist, possibly a later addition, lies to the N of the chamber, and has at one time been covered by an extension to the mound. Only a few stones left of the covering material remain. (On the rise NW of, and overlooking, the Benie Hoose.)

41 **Brough, Whalsay, cup-marked stone** 2 HU555651

Two groups of pecked cup-marks occur on the E side of a rock outcrop. There are at least 30 marks, in two groups. Such cup-marks, believed to be of Bronze Age date, are very rare in Shetland. (W of the road, 110m south of its right angled bend.)

42 **Ward of Symbister, Whalsay, chambered cairn** 2 HU533620

A rather ruinous cairn, with traces of a kerb, in a superb location. (Summit of hill, SW of ferry pier.)

43 **Battle Pund, Out Skerries, enclosure** 2 HU684713

This irregular setting of boulders, some 13m across, recalls Hjaltadans (Fetlar) (37), and may be of Bronze Age date. (Clearly visible to S of Sunnyside.)

44 ***Housetter, North Roe, chambered cairns** 3 HU362855

A sadly ruined cairn, with the facade facing E. The overall diameter has been about 9m, and the inner chamber, of trefoil plan, is 3m by 2 internally. The nearby Giant's Stones are the terminal orthostats of a similar cairn which has otherwise been completely scattered. High on the rocky hill to the W of the Giant's Stones is a very well preserved, but miniscule, chambered cairn (HU 360855). (To the W of the A970 road. The small cairn is a steep scramble and it requires patience to locate it.)

45 ***Ronas Hill, North Roe, chambered cairn** 3 HU305835

This, one of the best preserved chambered tombs in Shetland, stands on the summit of the highest hill in the islands. The chamber, which is built of large granite blocks, is still roofed, although much of the cairn material has been scattered over the surrounding slopes. Doubtless the chamber has survived because it provides a shelter in an exposed spot. The interior is rectangular, 1m by 1.25, and 1m high. A remnant of the entrance passage leads into the chamber, and this is the inner end of a formerly longer passage, which led from the outside of a cairn of about 15m in diameter. There is little trace of the outer edge of the cairn, which may have been round or heel-shaped in plan. (Via Collafirth Hill or the head of Ronas Voe. Not for the unfit or ill-shod.)

46 **Hamnavoe, Eshaness, standing stones** 3 HU243806

"The Giant's Stones" are a pair of upright slabs, one 1.8m tall, the other 2.4m. A third stone, recorded in 1774, has since vanished. The stones lie in an E to W line, but the significance of this is not clear. They may be sailing marks for the bay below. (N of the road, beyond Scarff.)

47 **Muckla Water, Eshaness, chambered cairn** 3 HU222788

This cairn, also known as the March Cairn, is an almost square example of the heel-shaped type. The remains of a facade can be seen on the N side, framed by uprights, but excavation proved that the small square chamber within was entered not from the facade but from the E side, a most unusual arrangement. (500m N of the junction of the B9078 and the Priesthoulland road.)

48 **Yamna Field, Gluss, standing stone** 3 HU334773

This tapering granite boulder, 1.6m high, stands on a western shoulder of the hill amid a litter of smaller blocks. Its location is not particularly prominent. (800m E of the A970 Hillswick junction.)

49 ***Punds Water, Mangaster, chambered cairn** 3 HU325713

This is the best surviving heel-shaped cairn on Mainland (only Muckle Ward on the uninhabited island of Vementry (53) survives better) and represents an extreme type of plan. The body of the cairn is 15m by 12, and has the outer ends of the facade prolonged into "horns" reminiscent of cairns in Caithness. Within the body of the cairn, and entered from a passage leading from the centre of the concave facade, is a small rectangular chamber with two alcoves. The main compartment is about 2m square. (750m NW from parking place on road just E of Mangaster, over a small hill.)

50 ***Islesburgh, chambered cairn** 3 HU693685

One of the finest heel-shaped cairns, this was excavated in 1959 and its plan is still very clear. It displays the classic semi-circular plan with concave facade. In front of the entrance passage are some stones wich may represent blocking dating from the abandonment of the cairn. The entrance passage leads into a roughly rectangular chamber. All of the slabs which would have roofed the passage and chamber have gone. (Overlooking the shore at Minn, to the W of Mavis Grind.)

51 ***Busta, Brae, standing stone** 3 HU349674

A huge monolith of granite, 3.2m high and about 1.6m wide and broad at the base, stands on the slope of the hill, near to another large block, which may have been a companion stone, now fallen. The Busta stone is a useful sailing mark, although surely far too large to have been erected for that purpose alone. (E of the road to Busta, and clearly visible from Brae.)

52 **Lunning, Lunnasting, standing stone** 3 HU506668

A 2m tall stone, of grey conglomerate. (Just beyond the public road's end.)

53 ***Muckle Ward, Vementry, chambered cairn** 3 HU295609

Perhaps the best-preserved heel-shaped cairn in Shetland, with diameter of just over 10m, this cairn displays the classic concave facade facing SE and a narrow entrance passage leading to a polygonal chamber. There are traces of two phases of building, with an original round cairn later elaborated to provide a heel-shaped plan. Interestingly, the entrance passage appears to have been sealed by the facade, suggesting the chamber was already out of use when the heel-shape was introduced. The facade is anchored at each end by rock outcrops. (Summit of hill 1km NWof landing place.)

54 **East Hill of Bellister, chambered cairn** 3 HU492592

A possible heel-shaped cairn, with a straight facade on the SE side and a few large stones, possibly indicating a chamber and passage, within a tumble of smaller stones 10m by 12. (On hillside, facing SE, 1km N of Housabister.)

55 **North Ward of Noonsbrough, chambered cairn** 3 HU292579

A mound of tumbled rubble marks the site of a heel-shaped cairn, the outer and inner kerbs defined by large blocks of stone and clear traces of a facade to the SE. A more recent watch-tower, now in ruins, lies above the likely location of the chamber of the cairn. (Summit of hill, 800m NNW from road end at Noonsbrough.)

56 **The Spinner, Sandness, cairn** 3 HU215562

This circular cairn, of 8m diameter, seem to have been bounded by a kerb of large blocks. A central cist, 1.4m by 1.1, can be seen, and is built of large slabs. This is probably a Bronze Age cairn, though any finds made when the chamber was dug out long ago have not survived. (On hilltop to E of road before it descends to Norby.)

57 ***Skellister, South Nesting, standing stone** 3 HU463552

A 3m tall standing stone, consisting of an irregular, pointed block of sandstone. Locally called "The Auld Wife", from its resemblence, in silhouette, to a stooped old woman. (Prominent, on a shelf above the junction of the main road and that for Skellister.)

58 **Cattapund Knowe, Sandness Road, long cairn** 3 HU247516

Under the walls of a group of sheep-pens lie the remains of a long cairn. This has been reduced to a single course of stones, and is somewhat less than impressive, but can be seen to have measured some 40m by 15. The long cairn may have been built by joining a pair of round cairns, and traces of a cist can be seen near the southern end. (Just W of junction of minor road from Walls to Sandness and A971 from Bridge of Walls to Sandness.)

59 **Gallow Hill, Walls, chambered cairns** 3 HU257507

A 10m diameter cairn, of round plan, with a large cist or ruined chamber in the centre. The central structure, and the edge of the cairn, are built of very large slabs. A second cairn lies to the E, of similar size but even more badly ruined. (Clearly visible to the N of the A971 road to Walls, 200m beyond the branch to Sandness.)

60 **Ward of Culswick, chambered cairn** 4 HU263462

The inner chamber and entrance passage can be seen within the rubble of this ruined cairn. (At north end of Vivilie Loch, 1km NW of Culswick chapel.)

61 **Wester Skeld, standing stone** 4 HU302433

This granite block, 2.8m high and up to 1.9m broad, is of particular interest due to the discovery nearby of a hoard of six polished stone knives of late Neolithic date. (On flattish open moorland, 500m S of summit of road from Easter to Wester Skeld.)

62 ***Murder Stone, Tingwall, standing stone** 4 HU412420

A stone 2m high, with a rectangular cross-section, stands immediately to the E of the road. There is a tale, probably recently invented, which relates a Norse tradition of a pardon for murderers who could run from the Law Ting Holm to the Murder Stone unscathed, against the efforts of the victim's family and friends. (E side of road between lochs of Asta and Tingwall.)

63 **Yaa Field, East Burra, standing stone** 4 HU378328

A block of gneiss, 2m high and 1m broad, but only 0.15m thick in places, this stone is visible for a considerable distance in most directions. (100m NE of Norbister.)

64 **Mid Field, West Burra, standing stone** 4 HU370326
Of similar height and material to the stone on Yaa Field (63) (which is visible from here), this upright slab is much thicker, being almost square in section. Local legend ascribes to the stone the quality of indestructability, a power which nature is slowly contradicting. (To the left of the road, S of Bridgend.)

65 **Ward of Scousburgh, chambered cairn** 4 HU388188
One of the few surviving prehistoric cairns in the South Mainland, this is a scattered mound of rubble, with clear traces of a kerb defining an original diameter of 9.5m. (On summit of hill, below trig point.)

66 ***Troswick, standing stone** 4 HU408166
A slab of sandstone 2.3m high, this stone stands close beside a field dyke, and may have functioned as a boundary marker, although it is hard to explain why, if this is the case, it is not incorporated in the nearby wall. Its size would suggest that it is of considerable antiquity, and has been used as a landmark, rather than erected to form one. (300m SSE of Troswick farm.)

67 **Hill of Cruester, Bressay, standing stone** 4 HU490428
A 3m high block of sandstone, with a distinct tilt. (Heogan road,then road past Keldabister, left onto track and follow this N.)

GAZETTEER: Bronze Age — burnt mounds

68 **Kettlester, Yell, 1 mound** 2 HU511800
One of the few burnt mounds in the North Isles, this example is still quite large, although much spread by agriculture. (Just S of the B9081 road at Kettlester.)

69 **Swainkatofts, Houbie, Fetlar, 1 mound** 2 HU632901
This small burnt mound is a fairly typical example. Like Unst and Yell, Fetlar does not appear to have many burnt mounds. (150m S of road, just past farm access.)

4 **Loch of Sandwick, Whalsay, 2 mounds** 2 HU538616
Within the settlement remains described above. (300-600m W of road, down hill from Sandwick crofts.)

A typical burnt mound, crescentic with a central stone trough, at Burnside, Hillswick.

70 ***Burnside, Hillswick, 1 mound**
3 HU281784
A mound of crescentic plan, some 11m across and up to 1m high. At its centre is a well-preserved cooking trough of stone, 1.4m long by 0.6m wide. (50m SW of house: ask for permission and take care with fences.)

71 ***Crosskirk, Eshaness, 1 mound**
3 HU215780
A large crescentic mound, with two stones of a probable trough visible. (Beside Loch of Breakon, S of the road to lighthouse.)

72 **Niddister, Hillswick, 1 mound**
3 HU278756
A large burnt mound, some 17m by 14m and 1.7m high, with the traces of a ruined cooking trough within the arms of the crescent. (At the W end of a small loch, S of Hillswick.)

73 **Lunna, Lunnasting, 2 mounds**
3 HU484697, HU485695
Two fairly undistinguished but typical burnt mounds, lying on rather damp ground. (The first lies 250m N of the second, which is beside the shore on the E side of West Lunna Voe.)

74 ***Crawton, Sandness, 1 mound**
3 HU214577
A very large burnt mound, of kidney-shaped plan, 16m by 12, and 1.5m high, this example stands beside a boggy area. There is no sign of a trough. (N of the roadside gate at the start of the track to Ness.)

75 **Noonsbrough, Clousta, 1 mound**
3 HU296573
A small example, looking almost like two separate mounds, set in a damp hollow. (In a dip SW of the end of the public road at Noonsbrough.)

76 **Huxter, Sandness, 2 mounds**
3 HU172565, HU173567
Two large burnt mounds are clearly visible from the shore of Loch of Huxter. These burnt mounds are unusual in having acquired names which are not purely locational: the Little and Muckle Brownie's Knowes. (SSW from the farm at Huxter.)

77 **Hockland, Stanydale, 2 mounds**
3 HU302513
Two mounds, both over 1.5m high, stand close together S of Hockland. (On the slope just S of Hockland.)

78 **Burn of Setter, Mid Walls, 5 mounds**
3 HU210503-HU214508
Five burnt mounds, all in a reasonable state of repair, can be seen scattered up the valley of the burn. (N of the main road, before a public telephone kiosk.)

79 ***Burraland, Walls, 1 mound**
3 HU223497
A large oval burnt mound stands close beside the deserted crofthouse. (S end of Loch of Burraland.)

80 **Grunivoe, Bridge of Walls, 3 mounds**
3 HU250488-HU252493
Three fairly typical specimens of burnt mounds, all part way between oval and crescentic in form, and all slightly damaged by grazing animals. (Respectively: beside the road to Whitesness; E of the road to Whitesness: in a slight valley running into the NW end of Loch of Grunnavoe.)

81 ***Upper Scalloway, Scalloway, 1 mound** 4 HU408402
This large mound has been rather scattered by agriculture and quarrying. It can be seen clearly from the main road. (At the junction of roads N of Scalloway, just W of the Tingwall road.)

82 **Mill Loch, Mousa, 1 mound** 4 HU460236
A much reduced burnt mound stands close beside a stream. It was originally of a horseshoe-shaped plan, but has now degenerated into two curved banks, whose concavities face each other across a central space within which can clearly be seen the edges of the slabs forming the cooking trough. (NE of the broch, at the W end of the Mill Loch - see Mousa broch (106) for access.)

83 ***Skelberry, Boddam, 4 mounds** 4 HU393163
These mounds lie along a shallow valley running N from the road. The largest, and nearest to the road, stands almost 3m high. (N of the B9122 Boddam to Bigton road, close to its junction with the main A970 road.)

84 **Backasetter, Boddam, 1 mound** 4 HU377156
A large crescentic mound stands in marshy ground, a typical location. (At S end of Loch of Spiggie, just N of a minor road.)

85 **Quendale, Sumburgh, 1 mound** 4 HU385128
An oval mound some 15m by 8 stands to 2m. It is near to the junction of two very small streams. (Leave main A970 road at junction for sandpit and walk downslope towards the back of the dunes in Quendale Bay. Mound is on lower slope of hill.)

86 **Cruester, Bressay, 1 mound** 4 HU483424
A large oval, 20m by 15, this burnt mound was excavated, partially, many years ago, and contained a small oval chamber with a corbelled roof. This was possibly part of a domestic building associated with the mound. (On the shore, NW of Gardie House.)

87 **Midgarth, Bressay, 1 mound** 4 HU500409
A large mound, but suffering from the trampling of livestock, this is of typical kidney-shape plan, and is about 11m long and 1m high. No trough is visible. (In the valley S of the road across the island, opposite the side road to Hoversta.)

88 ***Houlalie, Pund, Fair Isle, composite mound** 4 HZ377156
By far the largest burnt mound in Shetland, this measures 39m by 27, and stands to 3m in height. It has been dug into in the past, but there is no record of what, if anything, was discovered. The mound is composed of several separate smaller mounds, and probably had several cooking places. (On the gentle slope NE of Pund.)

Not all brochs survive as well as Burland, south of Lerwick.

89 **Underhoull, Unst, broch & ramparts** 1 HP574044

This ruined broch with strong outer defences stands on the edge of a steep slope. The sides not protected by the slope have been enclosed with two ditches, with massive earthen ramparts inside each. The back of the inner rampart is covered by rubble from the broch. The only feature of the broch which can be discerned is the outer end of the entrance passage, which is on the north, where a causeway runs through the ramparts, which are faced with stone in this portion of their circuit. (W of the road as it begins to descend into the Westing.)

90 ***Belmont, Unst, broch & ramparts** 1 HP557006

The broch is completely ruined, but around it is a most impressive set of defences. A deep ditch cuts off the angle of coast on which the broch stands. The inner face of this has been edged with a stone wall, which survives best at the western end of the ditch, beyond the approach causeway on that side. Beyond an outer rampart is a second, shallower, ditch. (Around shore to W of ferry terminal at Belmont.)

91 **Mula, Unst, house** 1 HU573999

A small oval house foundation is associated with clearance mounds and burnt stones, while nearby field banks

banks may be contemporary in date. The site has produced pottery of wheelhouse type, and illustrates the longevity of these simple oval houses in Shetland. (SE from Belmont ferry terminal, in the middle of the enclosed land of a long-abandoned croft.)

92 ***Burgi Geos, Yell, promontory fort**
1 HP478034

This remote site has one of the most spectacular locations of any in Shetland. A promontory formed by two narrow clefts in the cliffs has been cut off by an artificial ditch. Beyond the ditch can still be seen the remains of a dry stone structure, one wall showing of what may have been a blockhouse similar to that at Scatness. This wall runs right to the cliff edge on the northern side. On the landward side of the ditch, a pathway runs towards the fort, edged by upright stones set like teeth into a mound of earth. This appears to be a device called chevaux de frise, which is usually an extra defence, but here it seems to be intended to prevent those approaching from falling over the cliff. There are traces of fields and clearance cairns on the hill to the east, and these may well be contemporary with the fort. (On the uninhabited W coast of North Yell. A track runs from Gloup up Gloup Voe. From the head of the voe, the route lies W up Rule's Gill and over the moorland. Not for the unfit.)

93 ***Burra Ness, Yell, broch**
1 HU557957

Only the seaward portion of this broch has survived, but this still reaches 3m above ground level. At the S end of the visible remains is the wreck of a wallbase cell, perhaps once a guard cell. The broch has been protected on the landward side by a pair of earthen ramparts, and there are many small foundations within these. Behind the broch, the flat, rather boggy land is dotted with many clearance cairns. (Road to North Sandwick, then track S, then E, out to headland.)

94 **Aywick, Yell, promontory fort**
1 HU546873

This is a miniature bivallate fort, with three ramparts and two ditches. The ramparts stand up to 1.8m in height. The enclosed area has been somewhat eroded, but can never have been very large. So far as can be seen, the ramparts are made solely of earth and small stones. (1 km ENE of Aywick.)

95 **Snabrough, Fetlar, fort**
1 HU577933

This badly eroded fort has been claimed as a former broch site, on no good evidence. A last fragment of masonry, probably part of a blockhouse, is flanked on the shoreward side by two substantial banks and broad ditches. Pottery has been found in the shoreline section. (750m N of old ferry slipway at Brough Lodge.)

96 **Houbie, Fetlar, broch**
1 HU620903

The foundations of a broch, 18m in outer diameter, stand on a low platform flanked by a broad ditch and outer bank. A second bank is apparent on the NW side, where the approach is easiest. Some Medieval steatite workings lie 150m WSW of the broch. (200m S of road where it crosses West Burn of Houbie.)

97 **Aithbank, Fetlar, promontory fort** 1 HU642897

The promontory called Winna Tanga is crossed by three much-reduced rubble banks, and is almost certainly a promontory fort. (200m S of Aithbank.)

98 **Loch of Huxter, Whalsay, fort** 2 HU558620

An islet has been connected to the shore by a rubble causeway. Where the causeway reaches the islet, a small blockhouse, now ruined, once stood. This is recorded, last century, as standing over 2m tall, with an upper gallery in the wall. The rest of the islet is edged by a stone wall some 1.5m thick, and the join between it and the blockhouse suggests it was built after the blockhouse, although not necessarily long after. (On the S shore of the loch.)

99 ***Loch of Houlland, Eshaness, broch** 3 HU213793

This rubble-filled broch stands 2m above the encircling debris and probably to about 4m above its original ground level. The entrance is in the SW side, and has had a guard-cell on the right. Two ruined cells can be seen in the wall foundations. The promontory on which the broch stands has been cut off by a stone-faced bank. Within this enclosed area there are, as well as the broch, a number of oval and sub-rectangular foundations, some of which are later than the broch. A nearby island is joined to the shore and to the broch by causeways, and may have served as a place of safety for livestock. (N of the Eshaness road, leaving this 500m before the lighthouse carpark.)

100 **Burga Water, Lunnasting, dun** 3 HU481641

A small dun occupies an islet. Walling can be seen on the S and E sides. (At S end of loch, best approached by minor road to E.)

101 **Hog Island, North Nesting, promontory fort** 3 HU508581

This promontory fort has been cut off by the sea. Three ramparts are preserved on the landward side of a narrow channel, which has been eroded by the sea but was probably originally a natural dip. There is a central entrance gap in the ramparts. (At outer end of promontory, 700m E of Neap.)

102 ***Ness of Garth, Sandness, promontory fort** 3 HU216583

A promontory fort (which has been made into a tidal island by rising sea level) is protected by two stone-faced ramparts on the landward side. A less stoutly-built wall runs along the W side. There are small oval house foundations inside the fort, and these may be of later date, perhaps representing a monastic establishment. (Track leaves the public road by a gate just E of a telephone kiosk.)

103 ***Burga Water, Sandness Road, dun** 3 HU234539

Fine example of an island dun, preserved due to its inaccessibility. Partly tumbled stonework rings a small island, and survives well enough to suggest a circular plan and a wall 2m thick surrounding a 10m diameter interior. In places the wall stands 2m high. (Clearly visible to E of the A971 Sandness road as it crosses the E shoulder of Stourbrough Hill)

104 ***Culswick, broch** 4 HU253448

Two centuries ago this was the second highest surviving broch in Shetland, but has since been reduced to around 4m in height. The entrance can be seen on the SE side. There is a small chamber above the entrance passage, entered from within the broch, and a gallery has run within the wall at the same height as this chamber. A guard cell opens off the right hand side of the entrance passage. The blocky red granite of which the broch is constructed seems to have required unusual building techniques. A large triangular lintel over the outer end of the entrance passage seems to be designed to spread the load away from the rather poorly built passage roof, and instead of the more normal internal ledge or scarcement to support internal wooden structures and the roof, there are a series of protruding blocks spaced around the inside wall face about 3m above the original floor level. (On a hilltop, WNW of the ruined farm of Sotersta, W of Culswick.)

22 ***Clickimin, Lerwick, fort, broch & houses** 4 HU464408

An early Bronze Age unenclosed settlement consisting of a small oval house and outbuildings was replaced by a series of Iron Age defensive constructions before the site ended its use as a late Iron Age open settlement. The sequence of two or three partial rebuildings of a simple fort, with wooden lean-to buildings around its inner wallface, followed by the addition of a freestanding blockhouse, perhaps part of an uncompleted rebuilding of the defences, and finally a broch, is unique in northern Scotland. The subsequent disuse of the defensive elements was marked by a reduction of the diameter of the interior to form a single house, and the erection of a number of small sub-circular buildings within the fort wall but outside the broch. A possibly late, and potentially very important, feature is a stone slab set on the approach causeway across the marshy land outside the broch and marked with the carved shape of two footprints. Elsewhere in northern and western Britain such stones are often associated with kingship rituals. The site was excavated, badly, in the 1850s and again, to a higher standard, in the late 1950s and early 1960s. Guardianship monument, no charge. See also Historic Scotland guidebook. (Signposted, to right of A970 road leaving Lerwick for the S.)

105 ***Burland, Quarff, broch & ramparts** 4 HU445360

A broch with later internal structures stands on a promontory. To the landward side are three earthen ramparts, which were probably faced in stone. These are substantial enough to have constituted a defence on their own, and but for the broch this site would be classed as a promontory fort. The broch is remarkable in having its entrance less than 1m from the cliff edge, although this may be a product of later erosion. Within the broch are traces of later structures, similar to the arrangement at Clickimin (22) whereby the interior was narrowed to take a single house at ground level. (The easiest route, avoiding the worst of the boggy ground and fences, is from the A970 at Henry's Loch, S of Brindister, across the shoulder of moorland to the E and then N along the cliff edge.)

106 ***Mousa, broch** 4 HU456237

This is the best preserved broch in Scotland, and stands over 13m tall, little short of its original height. Although it was repaired in the mid 19th century, it was not heightened at this time. The base of the tower is unusually narrow, being just over 15m wide externally, with walls 4.5m, thick making Mousa the most massively built of any broch so far measured. The basal level is pierced by a narrow entrance, with no guard cells. In the wallbase are three oval cells, entered by narrow doorways from the central area. These have beehive corbelled roofs. The stairway starts at a raised aperture 2m above the broch floor and rises spirally through the hollow wall to the wallhead, where it opens onto a partially-roofed upper gallery. Within the double-skinned wall are six galleries, floored and roofed by lintels which also serve to tie the inner and outer walls together. These are difficult to reach from the stairway, as this cuts through them, necessitating a gap in each gallery floor. The inner face of the broch has long, vertical, gaps in the masonry, broken by spaced tie-stones. These "voids" allow light into the galleries, lighten the structure and may also have served, in conjunction with the two ledges which protrude from the inner face, to support a wooden structure of galleried form and a roof. On the floor of the broch is a rock-cut tank for water and a hearth, over which project the remains of a wheelhouse-like building which was inserted at a later date. Outside the broch are slight traces of outbuildings, contained within a stone wall which runs across the neck of the promontory on which the broch stands. Guardianship monument.

Charge for boat. See also Historic Scotland guidebook. (By boat from Sand Lodge, then 700m walk. Contact Tourist Office or telephone Sandwick 367 for details.)

107 **Southpunds, Levenwick, broch & house** 4 HU416198
Although now rather delapidated, this excavated broch is one of the four best-preserved in Shetland. The diameter is small, about 17m. The interior, 8m across, has been reduced by the insertion of a later circular house, which was entered through a gap broken through the broch at the level of the first gallery. The original entrance to the broch is visible on the NE, and to the right of it on entering a cell leads to a ruined stair. This ran up to the first gallery, which can be seen clearly, with a second flight of stairs rising from it on the S side of the broch. There is no trace of a second, higher, gallery which was recorded last century. The broch stands on a low platform, faced with masonry, and has been surrounded by two earthen ramparts, each of which has a cobble base. A small oval house stands to the W of the broch, within the ramparts. It is not clear from the excavation report if this house is earlier than the broch, as at Clickimin (22). (Downhill from the end of the road at Burgadies.)

108 **Clumlie, broch** 4 HU404181
This broch, revealed by excavation last century, stands in the centre of a group of croft buildings which are themselves of interest. The broch stands to just over 2m in height, and is of similar proportions to that at Jarlshof (26). Part of the outer wall has been removed. There is a guard cell to the right of the narrow entrance, while a cell on the left may have led to a stair. On the floor of the broch can be seen the outline of a hearth and stone subdivisions which may be original fittings of the broch, rather than later modifications. A later wall has been inserted, narrowing the interior diameter. (Within deserted croft, W of the road below Braefield.)

109 **Dalsetter, Boddam, broch & ramparts** 4 HU408157
Only a mound of rubble remains of the broch, but its surrounding ramparts are still impressive. Two earthen banks stand up to 3m tall, and between them is a broad flat-bottomed ditch. A gap in these defences, on the SE, probably marks the original approach. The remains form a prominent landmark for many miles, and the site is known as "da Brough", in preference to all the other local brochs, which are simply named after their locality. Whether this indicates an Iron Age importance, or simply the prominence of the site, is not known. (On the hilltop NE of Boddam.)

26 ***Jarlshof, Sumburgh, broch & houses** 4 HU399096
The broch lies at the centre of the coastal side of this complex site. It

has been neatly halved by marine erosion, and affords an unusual opportunity to see a broch in section. The remaining half of the broch stands well over 2m high. The outer diameter was 19m, with walls 5m thick at the base. The broch entrance passage has a guard cell, but any stair has gone with the vanished half of the structure. An outer wall, enclosing a courtyard around the broch entrance, was found to be contemporary with the broch, and was provided with an entrance containing a guard cell. This outer wall probably marks a stage of development beyond the ring-wall at Clickimin (22), and its occurence at the same date as a fully-developed broch may call into doubt the general applicability of the sequence at Clickimin. The complex of post-broch structures at Jarlshof is one of the most remarkable in Scotland. The broch was closely followed by a stone roundhouse, built within the outer enclosure of the broch. This was followed by three wheelhouses, one of which was built within the broch itself. Two of the wheelhouses survive almost intact, with roofs corbelled inwards to leave a small central hole which would have been easy to roof with thatch. These structures, so far as they can be dated by their form and finds, seem to have evolved on site, but the claim of the excavator that Jarlshof marked the point of birth of the wheelhouse architectural style seems hard to reconcile with the predominantly Hebridean distribution of this building form. The post-broch phase at Jarlshof is marked by rapid accumulation of wind-blown sand, in a series of layers, so that by the time of the early Pictish houses (see below) almost 2m had accumulated, and midden deposits had been built up to similar depths around the remains of the broch. The result is a very deep stratigraphy, and there are doubtless remains of many periods on this site, both in unexcavated parts and where the earlier excavators stopped at relatively late, high, levels. Guardianship monument, visitor centre, admission charge. See also Historic Scotland guidebook. (Signposted, parking at Sumburgh Hotel.)

110 **Scatness, Sumburgh, promontory fort** 4 HU388087

On the a headland north of Ness of Burgi (111) is a fort which was excavated in 1983. It proved to have a rectangular masonry blockhouse with a single oval cell in the surviving half, and an entrance passage with a door-check and a bar-hole halfway down. At the back of the blockhouse, protruding stones formed a stair, which was incorporated in a later modification which thickened the structure, perhaps to allow it to stand higher. On the landward side of the promontory is a rampart with a broad, irregular, ditch, the latter more like a quarry scoop than a defensive feature. (On E side of Scatness, 700m S from the end of the public road. Note: if parking here do not block the bus turning space.)

111 ***Ness of Burgi, Sumburgh, promontory fort** 4 HU388085
This is the classic example of a Shetland blockhouse fort. It was excavated in the 1930s and has been laid out for visitors. A double ditch with intervening rampart cuts off a promontory. A paved and stone-faced passage, possibly originally roofed, leads through this outer defence towards a rectangular block of masonry, pierced by a narrow entrance passage. A guard cell lies to the left of the passage, and two further cells lie to the right, entered from the rear of the blockhouse. The plan is interesting, for the blockhouse does not reach to the cliff edge on the N side, and there is no trace of a wall there. Also, no trace of any other buildings was found within the enclosed area, not even against the rear face of the blockhouse. It is thought that the blockhouse, which now stands about 2m high, was originally at least twice that height, with a wallhead walkway fronted by a parapet, but this is pure conjecture, based on the volume of tumbled stone removed by the excavators, and stacked neatly nearby. Guardianship monument, unrestricted access. See also Historic Scotland guidebook. (1km S of the end of the public road at Scatness. Note: if parking here do not block the bus turning space.)

112 **Noss Sound, Bressay, broch & ramparts** 4 HU528410
A large mound partly conceals the ruined broch. Traces of cells are visible within the walls. The mound is flanked by two substantial ramparts. These appear to be earthen, but recent marine erosion has shown that one, at least, conceals a stone-faced wall. The location is unusual for a broch, being overlooked by nearby high ground. (Park at the road end, and walk downslope to the Noss ferry point.)

113 **Grimsetter, Bressay, souterrain** 4 HU516395
This small souterrain, or earth-house, is a typical Shetland example, being small, cramped and hard to locate. It is frequently damp. (Track past W side of Loch of Grimsetter, to low saddle between the loch and the small valley of Seligeo.)

114 ***Landberg, Fair Isle, promontory fort** 4 HZ223722
A cliffed promontory is protected on the landward side by steep ramparts with intervening ditches, enclosing a small flat area, within which are the remains of at least one rectangular building of later date and slight traces of other structures. Rabbit-scrapes have produced late Iron Age pottery. (In front of the Fair Isle Bird Observatory building at North Haven.)

115 **Burgar Stack, Unst, eremitic site** 1 HP6611140

Slight traces of house foundations are located on this rock stack, which is linked to the shore by a dangerous rock ridge. (Do not attempt access, but view from the safety of the hill above. 800m E of Millfield, on E side of Kirkaton, Norwick.)

116 **Blue Mull, Unst, eremitic site**
1 HP557045
On a headland above steep cliffs may be seen seven oblong building foundations, arranged in a straight line. The headland has been delimited by a low bank, which seems unlikely ever to have been high enough to act as a defence. (1km NW of Lund Church.)

117 **Birrier of W. Sandwick, Yell, eremitic site** 1 HU438913
Facing Kame of Isbister (118) across Yell Sound, this almost inaccessible sloping promontory, linked to Yell by a rock ridge, has two rows of small dwelling foundations, and seems more likely to be an eremitic settlement than anything else, given its location. (Another site with dangerous access. It can be viewed from the nearby cliff edge. Track to Harkland, then NW to Birriesgirt Loch, then NW to the coast. The houses face seawards, and are hard to discern from the shore.)

118 ***Kame of Isbister, North Roe, eremitic site** 1 HU382915
On a steep slope above Yell Sound are the remains of 23 small sub-rectangular foundations, each one about 3m by 6m. They are arranged in two rows. (The only approach is by a crumbling rock ridge, and is not recommended. E from Isbister

The puzzling foot-marked stone at Clickimin may be a relic of Pictish rituals.

to a small loch, then along the clifftops, which give a good view of the location, but the houses face seawards, and cannot be seen from the shore.)

22 ***Clickimin, Lerwick, fort, broch & houses** 4 HU464408

The last phases at this site are arguably Pictish rather than late Iron Age, in so far as the two can be separated. See above for description.

119 **Papil, West Burra, church site** 4 HU368315

The post-Reformation church at Papil, itself rapidly falling into ruin, stands on a low mound which represents the site of at least one earlier church, dedicated to St Laurence. This, together with the church on St Ninian's Isle (120), may have been one of the principal churches of southern Shetland in pre-Norse times and possibly later. Nothing can be seen on site from this period apart from a curved bank which may be part of an enclosure associated with the early church. The churchyard has produced a remarkable group of Pictish sculptured stones which seem to span a long period of time. Among the early pieces is the "Papil Stone", a cross slab bearing an incised pattern including a lion and two bird-headed men, and equally impressive is the side slab of an altar or shrine which depicts a procession of four clerics, one mounted on a small horse. This is probably the earliest known depiction of a Shetland pony. A number of other fragments suggest that, in its original form, this site was a circular enclosure with a small chapel towards the centre and several open-air shrines dotted about the churchyard. There may well be more remaining on this site than is apparent, for the level of the ground has built up since the period in which the first church was built, perhaps as early as the eighth century. (To the W of the public road, at Papil. Still in use as a burial ground.)

120 ***St Ninian's Isle, Dunrossness, church site** 4 HU368208

The ruins of the church on this island overlie an earlier one, within the floor of which was found the famous St Ninian's treasure, a collection of many items of Pictish silverware: bowls, brooches and other ornaments. The earliest use of all appears to have been as an Iron Age farmstead, although almost all traces of this period were destroyed by subsequent ecclesiastical building. The first church was a simple rectangular chapel in a circular enclosure. Associated with it were some finely carved stones in the Pictish style, including a post-and-slab shrine lying S of the chancel. The later church, the ruins of which can be seen, is probably twelfth or thirteenth century in date. It is worth noting that the stone-lined pit within the ruins is not the site of the treasure discovery, but merely shows the depth of the floor of the primary chapel below the later one. Although there is little documented history for this site it must have been one of the principal churches in pre-Norse Shetland. Recently there has been some reconsideration of the Ninianic dedication, formerly believed to be a late one. The church was recognised as a holy place long after its disuse, and disapproving ministers of the reformed church wrote of candles being lit at the ruined altar. (Signposted track from Bigton, parking above the shore, then across the beach. The chapel is NW of the point where the beach reaches the island.)

26 ***Jarlshof, Sumburgh, houses**
4 HU399096

After the wheelhouses, at the beginning of the Pictish period, a series of sunken-floored, sub-circular houses was built. These are associated with two small souterrains, or earth-houses, which were probably underground stores. The houses may have been built of turf, with only stone foundations. Even later is a small house with a kiln-barn, which stands to the W of the main complex. A group of poorly-preserved circular houses lay directly under the later Norse settlement (see below) but these are not visible on the site as laid out. These houses may have been inhabited at the date of the first Norse incursion. Guardianship monument, visitor centre, admission charge. See also Historic Scotland guidebook. (Signposted, parking at Sumburgh Hotel.)

121 **Cullingsburgh, Bressay, church site**
4 HU522423

The remains of a cruciform church, dedicated to St Mary, lie within an old graveyard. The much reduced foundations of a broch lie under the NW corner of the graveyard. A very fine Pictish cross-slab from here has one of the few ogham inscriptions so far found in Shetland. (Road to Setter, then 700m track along shore to E.)

GAZETTEER: Viking/Norse

122 **Underhoull, Unst, house**
1 HP573044

Downhill from the broch (89) are the ruins of early Norse houses excavated in the 1960's, but now falling into disrepair. The houses here lay above a Pictish period settlement of round houses. (200m downhill from Underhoull broch.)

123 **Sandwick, Unst, house**
1 HP618023

A late Norse, rather than a Viking, house, this ruined rectangular farmstead dates to around 1300 AD,

From the air the stone-built causeway leading across the marsh to the Law Ting Holm is visible as a line leading from the left edge of the photograph.

but in its location at the back of the beach and its layout, with a main building and nearby byre, all within an enclosed yard, it reflects the Norse influence on later Shetland farm arrangements which began with the Viking settlement. The site was excavated in the late 1970s. One of the most interesting features was a "cow-shaped" doorway aperture, narrow at the bottom and widening upwards. This finally explained the problem that the foundation dimensions of the doorways of excavated Norse byres always seemed to narrow for cattle to pass through. A Pictish period burial was found nearby, below a rectangular cairn of quartz pebbles. (Road to Hannigarth, then 500m N, gently downhill to the S end of the bay.)

33 **Breakon, Yell, burial**

1 HP528053

Near to a rather ruinous oval house, probably prehistoric, is a pointed-oval, or boat-shaped, setting of flat slabs protruding from the sandy soil. This may be the remains of a Viking-period burial, although the local traditions of burial nearby appear to be associated with the rather larger mounds nearer the shore. (Follow track from Breakon Farm.)

124 **Gossabrough, Yell, houses**

1 HU534833

To the N and E of the mound formed by a ruined broch are the remains of rectangular structures which may be early Norse dwellings. If this is the case, the settlement may be as extensive as that of Jarlshof.

(Beyond the farm buildings at Gossabrough.)

125 **Strandburgh, Fetlar, monastic site** 1 HU670930
This monastic site, of probable Norse date, has two elements, which were possibly once linked by a bridge or a natural causeway. On the Outer Brough, a detached stack, are the remains of long houses with slightly bowed walls. The buildings on the stack may represent the monastic centre, while similar ones on the main island may represent a farm which would have helped support the community. Remains of small buildings also exist upon the Clett (HU 642945), an almost inaccessible stack 3km to the W. These may have formed a hermitage founded from the main centre, and used as a retreat for solitary contemplation. (Road to Everland, then NNE to end of island.)

126 **Giants Grave, Aith, Fetlar, burial** 1 HU638899
A possible pagan Norse grave is represented by an oval mound of stones some 10m by 5. (Overlooking Wick of Aith, on the W side of the bay.)

127 **Kirk Holm, Sand, monastic site** 4 HU337460
Another site, like Kame of Isbister (118) or Birrier of West Sandwick (117), with a row of buildings, but here the structures are much larger, being up to 11m in length. They stand parallel, end-on to the shore. This seems most likely to be a Norse period site, similar to the Peerie Brough, Birsay, Orkney, rather than a very early settlement of Pictish date. (In voe to E of road to Reawick, the site lies at N end of islet.)

128 ***Law Ting Holm, Tingwall, thingstead mound** 4 HU417435
The mound at the N end of the loch is traditionally pointed out as the meeting place of the senior legislative assembly for all of Shetland, in the years preceding the Scottish takeover of the islands. An artificial causeway leads through marshy ground to a natural knoll, which is almost surrounded by water. Such a location, where the deliberations of the assembly could be seen but not necessarily overheard, is typical of thingstead sites throughout the N Atlantic area. (E of the road, at the N end of Tingwall Loch - Tingwall means "the valley of the thing, or parliament".)

129 ***Burn of Catpund, Cunningsburgh, quarries** 4 HU426272
Some fine examples of soapstone working, with chisel-marks preserved on many faces. Most, if not all, of the visible working is medieval rather than Viking in date. A small area of carved rock has recently been exposed, and shows to good advantage the intensive nature of the working of the rock face. (About 1km up the bed of the first burn of any size S of South Brig of Cunningsburgh, just beyond a well-surfaced branch road to the W of the A970.)

26 ***Jarlshof, Sumburgh, houses**
4 HU399096

The extensive Viking period and later remains represent a long sequence of habitation, from the first Norse settlement through a later village and medieval farm, and ending with a substantial dwelling of late 16th century date. The original settlement seems to have been of one or more very large long halls, which were subsequently modified, sub-divided and added to, resulting in a warren of buildings. It is very difficult to understand the Viking-Norse sequence from the remains as laid out on site. Guardianship monument, visitor centre, admission charge. See also Historic Scotland guidebook. (Signposted, car parking at Sumburgh Hotel.)

From ground level the Law Ting Holm's topography fails to match its important historical significance.

SEVERAL tours, based on the use of a car, are described below. Each should take even the most interested visitor less than a full summer's day to complete. Tours marked * could be done by a keen walker in a day, given transport to, or accommodation at, the start and finish. Sites which are described in the Gazetteer section have their number in brackets, others have their six-figure Ordnance Survey grid reference.

Lerwick and Scalloway

Commencing from Lerwick, take the main A970 road S, signposted for Sumburgh. Clickimin (22), a complex site with a prehistoric house, a fort and a broch, is on the right opposite the petrol station at Sound. Continue on the main road to the public hall at Sound, From here it is a 1km walk S along the slope of the hill to the ruined prehistoric house at Punds Geo (23). Back on the road, a further 4km S to the parking area beside the Loch of Brindister on the right, with a small circular dun on an island (HU433370). To the E, silhouetted against the sea, is the Broch of Burland (105). It is possible to reach the broch from here, down the Brindister Burn, which has some fine ruined watermills, but the route can be very damp, and there are many fences to cross. A more reliable route is to continue S to the small Henry's Loch, on the right of the road, and walk from here, along the moorland ridge and then N up the coast, about 1km each way.

Back at the car, retrace one's direction, N up the main road and then onto the B9073 road to Scalloway. Stop on the hill overlooking Scalloway for a fine view of the village and the late sixteenth-century castle (HU404392). Scalloway has a small

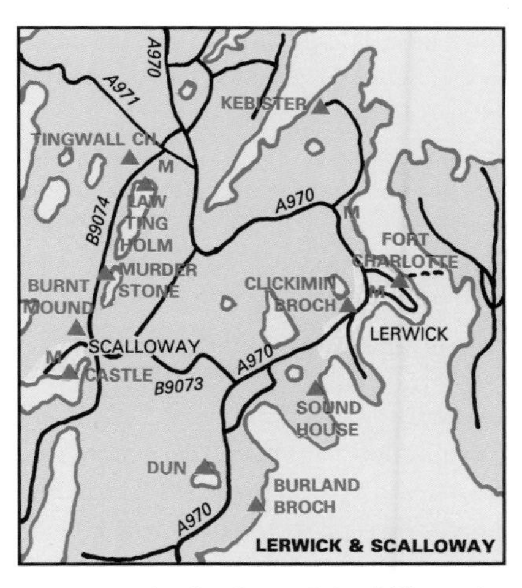

museum. At the foot of the hill, to the right of the road just beyond the road for Tingwall, is a large burnt mound (81). The large modern house on the hilltop behind is built beside the site of a broch, excavated in the early 1990's.

After visiting Scalloway, take the Tingwall (the name means parliament valley) road, the B9074. The Murder Stone (62) is passed on the right after 2km. A further 2km and the Law Ting Holm (128), site of the Medieval Norse assembly for the islands, can be seen in the N end of the Loch of Tingwall. The church on the left (HU419438) is on an old site, and in Medieval times was probably one of the chief churches in Shetland. A Medieval burial vault with some interesting gravestones survives. The whole Tingwall area is central to the later history of Shetland, with the former capital of Scalloway at the S end and the fertile soils of the limestone-rich valley making it very desirable farmland.

Turn right at the Tingwall crossroads onto the A971, passing a farm museum on the right (HU428443), and climb the hill to join the A970 from the N. Follow this back towards Lerwick, passing on the left, just entering Lerwick, a restored late medieval trading booth and house, the Bod of Gremista (HU464432). A side road to the left leads out to Kebister (HU458454), where, beyond a new oil-rig servicing base (often inactive) are the remains of a Medieval teind (tithe) barn which belonged to the Archdeacon of the islands. Entering the town, the fine artillery fortification, Fort Charlotte, is on the right (HU475424). This was built to counter threatened French raids. In the town, on Lower Hillhead, is the Shetland Museum, with a fine collection of artefacts of all periods and some fascinating later exhibits, emphasising the importance of such materials as straw, wood and heather, which tend not to survive on archaeological sites.

* Cunningsburgh and Sandwick

Starting at the South Brig of Cunningsburgh (HU428281), note the churchyard of Mail to the left, above the shore, where a recent find of a Pictish stone was made (HU433279). Drive S on the A970 and park near the access to a quarry on the steep hill to the left. A path leads from here up the Catpund Burn (129), with the finest steatite outcrops in Shetland, showing the hollows made by carving out bowls. The stream has also carved out the soft stone to give some unusual forms to its course.

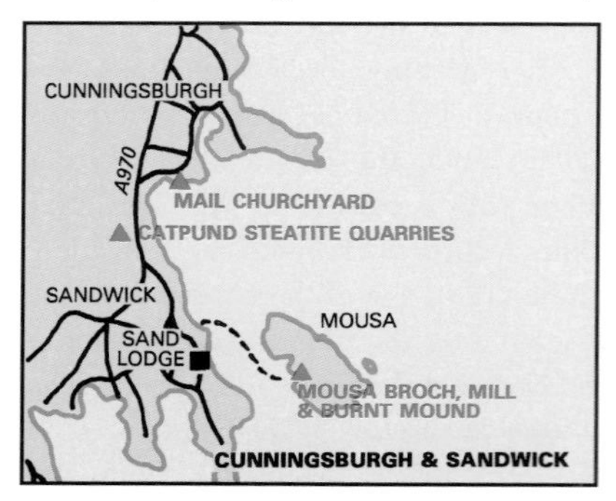

Continue S, turning off to Sand Lodge (HU436249), signposted for Mousa. The boat is scheduled in summer, or by prior arrangement (telephone Sandwick 367). On the island, the landing place is by a small shepherd's hut, and the path leads over a shoulder of hill to give a fine view of the broch (106), and behind it the ruined laird's house, or "haa". A ruined mill is passed in a marshy area en route for the broch, and further up this small stream is a burnt mound. There are some interesting ruined crofts on the island. The boat returns to Sand Lodge, near which are the slight remains of a copper mine, which was worked intermittently over several centuries but never to any great profit.

Start at Levenwick cemetery (HU414 213), which although not recorded as an ancient church site has a mounded, oval shape strongly suggestive of many centuries of burials. It is possible to walk from here down the coast to Southpunds broch, but a shorter walk is obtained by taking minor roads to the road end at Southpunds. Southpunds broch (107), also called Levenwick, was excavated last century, but has since become rather delapidated.

Joining the A970 road, drive S for a short distance and then branch left to Clumlie (108). The broch here is set in the middle of a deserted croft, with the house and outbuildings constructed around what was then a large mound, and only subsequently revealed itself as a broch. The placename, Clumlie, is believed by some to derived from Columb-chille, the Gaelic form of Columba. If this is correct, it would be one of the very few Gaelic-derived placenames, perhaps the only one, in Shetland. Continuing S on the minor road, there is a fine group of Norse mills on the burn coming out of Loch of Clumlie, and between the road and the loch remains of a sluice arrangment (HU404173). On the S side of the stream valley, overlooking the bay of Troswick, is a standing stone (66). Again, the placename is of interest: Troswick means "trolls' bay".

S again, the site of the broch at Dalsetter (109), with its outer ramparts, forms a prominent skyline feature to the left. Between the broch and the road is a prehistoric settlement, with the remains of three small oval houses, field walls and

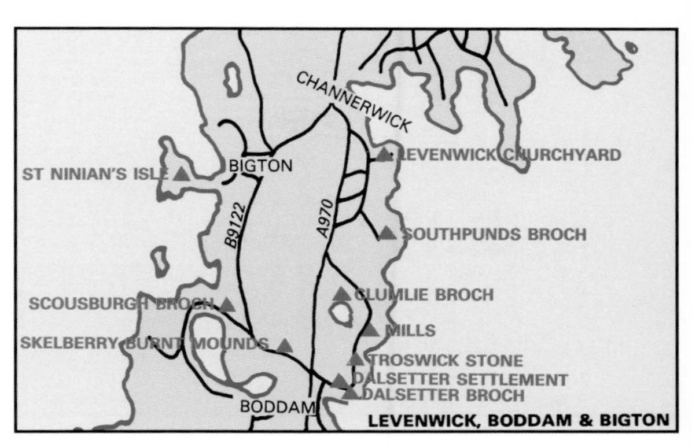

clearance cairns. Follow the road onwards to Boddam, passing an interesting eighteenth-century merchant's house with upper-floor store reached by an external stair (HU398155).

Rejoin the main road and almost immediately leave it, following signs for Bigton on the B9122. On the right is one of the Skelberry burnt mounds, in a typical valley-bottom location (83). Further on, just before a small garage, a large mound on the left conceals the broch of Scousburgh (HU377178). The road turns N, with views of typical small farms and crofts, with remnants of the old strip-fields. Follow signs down to Bigton, and then to St Ninian's Isle. There is a good car-park at the foot of a track leading down to the beach, the finest example of a sand tombolo in Britain. The chapel site (120) lies on the island, and it is a pleasant walk across the beach followed by a scramble up the sandy slope on the far side. Bird watchers will find puffins on the far (W) side of the island during the breeding season. The B9122 through Bigton leads N to the main A970 road at Channerwick (HU398155).

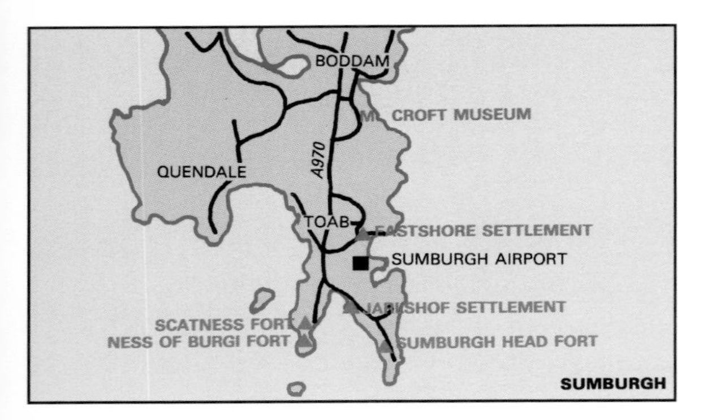

Starting from the Airport, follow the main A970 road and signs to the complex site of Jarlshof (26), which is probably the most long-lived settlement site ever excavated in Scotland, with a start in the Bronze Age and an end in the seventeenth century AD. During the summer months, when the visitor centre is open, there is a charge for admittance. Overlooking the site at Jarlshof is Sumburgh Head, and the much-reduced ramparts of a fort can be seen where the road passes through the wall around the lighthouse there (HU407080). The name, Sumburgh, may be derived from Swein-borg, "Swein's fort".

Follow the A970 N to the junction for Scatness, and turn down to the S. At the road end, park carefully so as not to cause an obstruction, and walk down over open salt-stunted grassland to the forts of Scatness (110), partly excavated in 1983, and beyond it (be careful on the rocky ridge leading across to it) Ness of Burgi, the classic Shetland blockhouse fort, excavated in the 1930s and now consolidated and cared for by Historic Scotland (111). Back on the A970, drive past the end of the main runway, noticing on the headland beyond the bay the multi-period site of Eastshore (HU403113). Unexcavated, this may well be just as complex as Jarlshof. It contains at least a broch, Norse remains and medieval houses, and late Neolithic finds have been made from the eroding shore section. Over the hill on the A970, turn right to Southvoe, to visit the Shetland Croft House, a fine refurbished thatched croft-house, with nearby a reconstructed working Norse-type mill (HU398146).

* Bressay

Take the ferry to Maryfield on Bressay. Take the road S to the school and post office, the E up the hill into the centre of the island. Branch left, signposted for Setter. (A fork to the left leads towards Aith, beyond which a fine walk leads N to Score Hill (HU513448), with a World War I gun emplacement, complete with gun. There are many traces of wartime in Bressay, mainly the concrete foundations of Nissen huts, sometimes with their brick-built chimney stacks still upright.) Keep on the road to Setter, park where the road runs out and follow the rough track to the church and broch site at Cullingsburgh (121).

Return to the main road, and turn sharp left towards the Noss ferry. The concrete tower on the hilltop (HU524415) is a lookout point associated with the gun emplacements at the N and S ends of the island. Park at the road end, and walk down to the shore, past the large mound marking the remains of Noss Sound broch (112). During the summer a ferry is operated to Noss by Scottish Natural Heritage, by whom the island is managed as a Nature Reserve, of particular interest for the seabirds which nest on the cliffs. There is little of great archaeological merit on Noss, except the traces of a chapel by the warden's house and visitor centre at Gungstie (HU531410), and a rather unexciting burnt mound on the SW shore of the island (HU539401). Noss' chief historic site is the beautifully restored pony stud farm at Gungstie (HU531411), recalling the days when the island was used for breeding Shetland ponies for use in the mines of the Scottish and English coalfields.

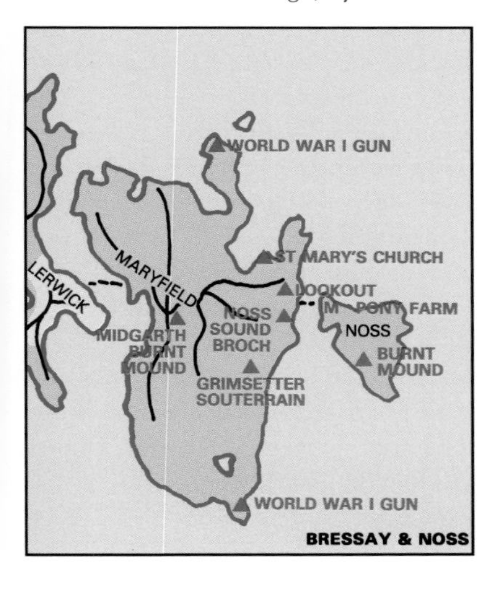

Return to Bressay, and follow the road directly back across the island. A detour to the S leads to Grimsetter, where a little searching reveals a small souterrain (113). To the left of the road as it runs downhill towards the east shore is a fine burnt mound at Midgarth (87). Return to Lerwick by the ferry.

Whiteness, Weisdale and Nesting

Start on the A971 beside the old schoolhouse at the junction for South Whiteness (HU392467). There is a burnt mound just down the South Whiteness road. To the NE, in the middle of the Loch of Strom, are the remains of an early rectangular castle, perhaps dating to the days of the Sinclair Earls in the 14th or 15th century (HU395476). The ruins are accessible at low tide by a causeway, for the brackish loch is slightly affected by the tides. Continue N on the A971, passing on the right and then on the left two silver workshops. The second, on the left, uses some of the rock-types used by Neolithic axe-makers, although for the less warlike purpose of polished stone jewellery.

Across the inlet of the sea to the left of the road, on the E slope of Hill of Olligarth, can be seen a cleared area surrounded by a tumbled stone wall, and at the centre of this are the remains of a prehistoric homestead (HU388473). At the very head of the inlet, Stromness Voe, is a good burnt mound (HU389477). As the road runs N, across the next inlet, Weisdale Voe, can be seen

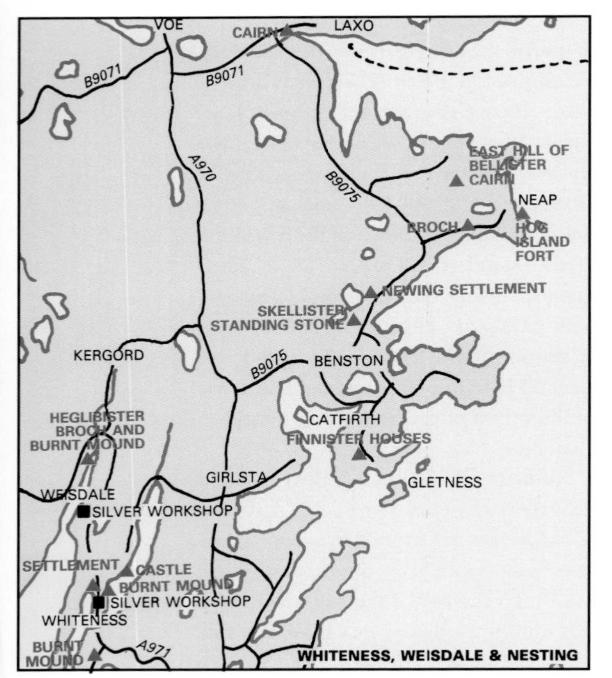

the old house, chapel and graveyard at Sound (HU383501), and, N of this, a prominent green bump level with the croft at Heglibster (HU388516) is believed to conceal the remains of a broch, while between it and the water is another burnt mound.

Take the B9075 branch road from the head of Weisdale Voe, through the trees (a rarity in Shetland) at Kergord (HU395 542) and over the central ridge of Mainland at Lamba Scord. Join the A970, turning right and then, after 2km, left on the B9075 towards Nesting, passing first through Catfirth (HU440540), which was a wartime flying-boat base. Turn right towards Benston, and take the road towards Gletness. Stop overlooking the shore and walk SW, past the abandoned croft of Finnister, to locate the two prehistoric houses on the hillside shoulder beyond (13). The whole area of South Nesting is rich in small burnt mounds and other interesting green bumps, some archaeological but many the result of limestone quarrying. Leaving South Nesting by the N road, at Skellister the fine standing stone called "The Auld Wife" overlooks the area (57).

The road to North Nesting now passes among the houses at Newing (12). Two oval houses lie level with the road on the right, one lies to the left and a fourth lies well below the road on the right. Traces of walls and cairns, and a small burnt mound, can all be seen here. At the memorial at Brettabister, turn right. Pass Housabister, before which the foundations of a broch can be found just behind the chapel (HU487578), and drive to Neap, at the road end.

Park carefully, and walk E to the headland, where at Hog Island Sound a promontory fort has been bisected by the sea (101). The chambered cairn of East Hill of Bellister (54) lies halfway up the SE-facing slope of the hill above Neap, about 1km from the end of the public road.

Continue to Laxo (which means "salmon river"), where a fine waterfall may be seen in the Laxo Burn, especially when the burn is in spate. A rather featureless mound beyond the burn may be a ruined cairn or a burnt mound with a lot of large stones in its composition (HU445635). Turn W, towards Voe, and end the tour with a visit to this pleasant little village at the end of Olna Firth, with its slightly Norwegian appearance.

Start on the A971 at the Bixter shop and post office (HU332523). Take the Aith road, the B9071, soon branching off towards Clousta. After 4km, just approaching the first houses at Clousta, there is a small oval prehistoric house and field to the left: the road actually cuts through the field wall (HU314569).

Continue to the end of the road at Noonsbrough. There is a good burnt mound (75) just across the fence. Follow a track SW across the hill for just less than 1km to the bay at Point of Hurds, where in the valley there is a small house and another mound, perhaps a large cairn or a very ruined house, and a few clearance cairns (HU289568). Walk N, keeping well up the rather steep hillside, dropping down past the remains of a chambered cairn on a hillside shoulder to the little loch before the promontory of Longa Ness. An oval house lies below a stone-built sheep shelter, and a second house lies about 100m to the E. Around these, especially the E one, is an extensive field system, with some quite large clearance cairns (11).

Climb ENE to the summit of North Ward of Noonsburgh, where a modern cairn surmounts a ruined heel-shaped one (55), and then head SE, dropping quickly. There is a fine view from above of the remains of Noonsbrough broch, which stands on a small island that has become linked to the shore by two shingle beaches (HU295576). The broch is largely concealed by the walls of more recent buildings.

Rejoin the road, and return to Bixter. (Those on foot can cut across the moor from Greenmeadow, past a standing stone (HU325558), to pick up the Aith road at Haarwell.)

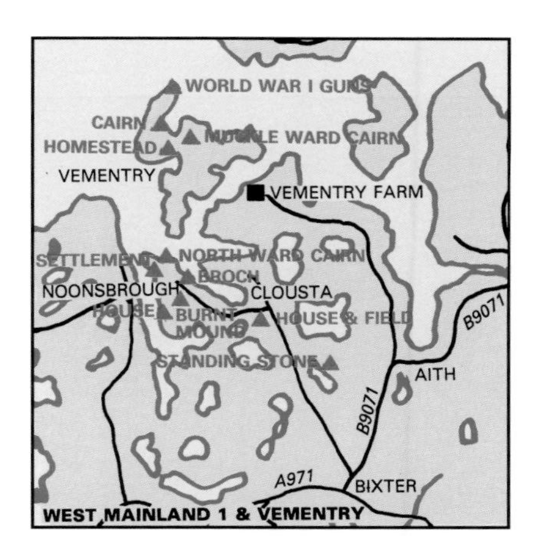

West Mainland 2

Start on the A971 at the large white house to the N of the road at Park Hall (HU313527) (there is a ruined chambered cairn on top of the small hill behind the house). Take the B9071 S past Garderhouse. To the S, where Seli Voe meets the sea, the small island of Kirk Holm has the remains of a possible monastic site on the E side of its N end (127).

The road crosses the hill to Easter Skeld, which is overlooked from the W by a chambered cairn (HU305450), best approached from the highest point of the road beyond the settlement. Further S, reached by detouring S from Easter Skeld on a minor road, a fine standing stone crowns a low hill (61). Follow the B9071 and then the branch road to Culswick (HU272450).

Park, and take the track over the hill past a small chapel. Follow a newly-bulldozed track out round the N side of Loch of Sotersta. As this comes towards the sea, there is a good view across a small loch to the broch of Culswick (104). There is a recent stone-built causeway across the N end of the loch, leading towards the broch, which is built of red granite and is one of the tallest unexcavated brochs in Shetland, with a striking triangular lintel over the entrance. To return, cross the S end of the loch and then a low rise to reach the deserted settlement of Sotersta (HU262446), where a standing stone is built into the corner of a ruined barn. A burnt mound lies beside the stream nearby. Head NE, following a rough track, back to the chapel at Culswick and regain the road.

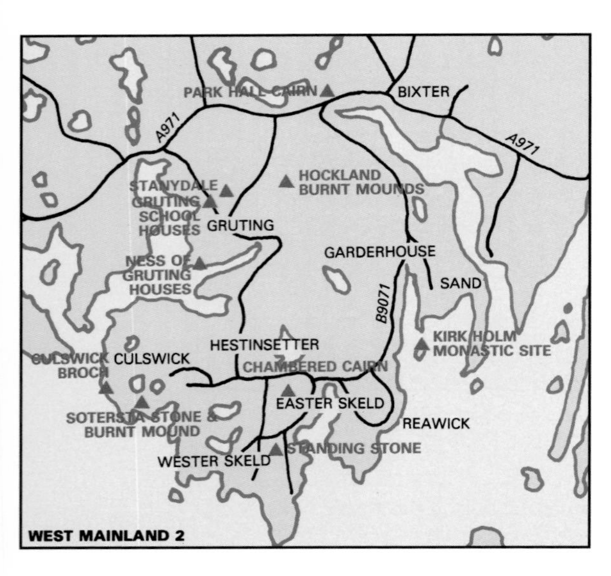

Branch N on the minor road at Hestinsetter, passing Olas Voe and Seli Voe (there are several rather ruined chambered cairns in this area), to the crossroads at Gruting (HU286495). Branching left and on to the Gruting road end, and then walking S, brings one to the prehistoric houses and fields at Ness of Gruting (20). Heading straight on one comes to the houses at Gruting School (19). However, if time is wearing on, the one essential visit is to Stanydale (18).

Turn right and after 1km park by the roadside sign, From here it is a gentle 700m across the moor, marked by posts, to the remarkable ''temple'', or hall, at Stanydale, with its attendant upright stones and remains of houses and fields. One of the houses was excavated in the 1940s, and lies beside one of the marker posts.

Return to the road, and drive N (the burnt mounds at Hockland (77) lie across the valley to the E) to regain the A971 1km W of Park Hall.

West Mainland 3

Start at Brig (Bridge) of Walls (HU260512). Take the A971 Sandness road (note that the A971 branches, with forks leading both to Walls and to Sandness: take the latter) stopping on the shoulder of the hill to visit the excavated settlement at Scord of Brouster (15). To the W, at the road junction, is the ruined long cairn at Cattapund Knowe (58). This requires great faith to discern amongst a tumble of stone. 1km further along the road, the area to the right called Trolligarts (14) (just to the E of the "chambered cairn" legend on the map, the name means "trolls' yards", or "trolls' fields") is a complex of prehistoric and more recent walls. Below abandoned sheep-pens and cabbage patches can be identified the sites of at least two oval houses, but the whole area feels rather more promising than the identifiable remains warrant, and would merit thorough survey. Neither of the cairns marked on the map is particularly impressive.

Back on the A971, continue NW. There is a ruined dun (a small, lightweight broch) in Burga Water to the right (103). The road twists through peaty moorland, then begins to fall towards the fertile area of Sandness. On the right at the top of the hill is the large cairn called The Spinner (56).

Turn right towards Bousta, stopping in a dip just beyond a public telephone kiosk, beside a gate giving access to a track on the left. A splendid burnt mound (74), one of Shetland's best, stands in a boggy area, and the track leads out, past some ruined mills, to the headland of

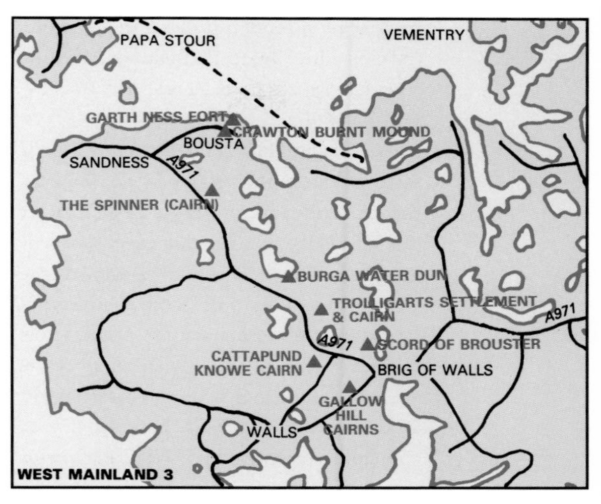

Ness, where a short scramble over a rocky beach gives access to the promontory fort of Ness of Garth (102). Like several such forts, this one has small oval foundations on it which may be later houses, perhaps of monastic origin.

Return along the same road, turning right at Cattapund Knowe to the village of Walls (HU245495), which was once a thriving herring port, and still has remains of piers, wharves and a ruined fish-oil factory. (The village bakery makes superb oatcakes.) Return along the main road to the starting point at Brig of Walls, passing on the left two rather large but almost totally ruined chambered cairns at the foot of Gallow Hill (59).

* Vementry

From Aith (HU343553) take the road to Vementry farm (HU308597), and by prior arrangement (through Tourist Office in Lerwick) hire boat to island of Vementry. On the highest hill of the island, Muckle Ward, is the best-preserved chambered cairn in Shetland (53). To the SW, at the head of Northra Voe, is a ruined homestead (HU293608), and N of this, at the foot of the hill, a ruined cairn (HU289612). Well worth visiting if on the island is the coastal defence battery on Swarbacks Head (HU290619). Two naval guns survive, together with their underground magazines and lookout post, from their installation in 1917 to protect the approaches to Swarbacks Minn, which sheltered a cruiser squadron during the First World War. They are among the youngest of "ancient monuments", having been given legal protection in 1992.

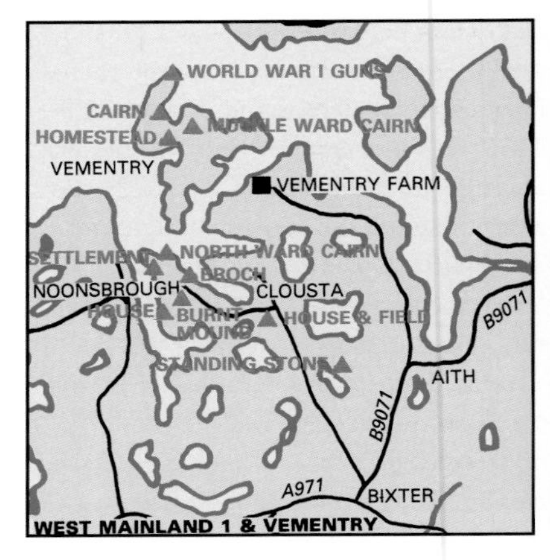

* Hillswick and Eshaness

Starting at Hillswick (HU282750), at the end of the west branch of the A970, walk SW from the S end of the public road to the small prehistoric house at Grevasand (7), which lies high on a shoulder near to spectacular cliffs. Head SE to a small loch at Niddister (72), with a substantial burnt mound at the W end of the loch. Return to Hillswick.

From Hillswick take the A970, then the B9078 for Esha Ness. At Burnside (70) there is a fine burnt mound, and after passing the small house at Black Water (6), also to the right of the road take the right fork for Esha Ness lighthouse.

(The main road, to the left, leads after a short distance to Stenness, a beautiful bay with remains of a nineteenth century fishing station (HU215772).) Another burnt mound lies to the left, by the loch at Cross Kirk (71).

Follow the right hand road almost to the lighthouse, then strike NNE across short cliff-top grass to the broch at Loch of Houlland (99).

There are ruined mills on the stream that drains the loch into a collapsed cave, the Holes of Scraada (HU213793). The cliffs here are spectacular, and a good watching point for puffins and other seabirds in the summer.

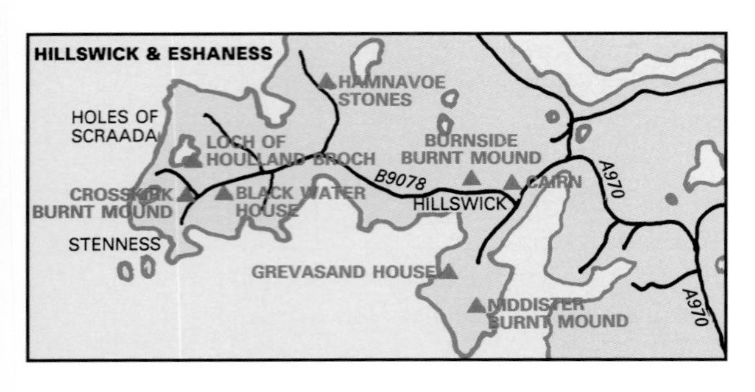

Park at the end of the north branch of the A970 at Isbister (HU371909). Head E up a small burn to a loch, and then follow the top of the cliffs N to obtain a good view of the spectacular monastic settlement at Kame of Isbister (118). Return to the road end. (There is a very interesting ruined fishing station of nineteenth century date at Fedaland (HU374942), 3.5km N along a private track from the road end.)

Drive S on the A970 to North Roe. Park near the school (HU364896), and take a recently improved, but still rough, hill track W to the N facing slope above Mill Loch, the Beorgs of Uyea (5), where there are many traces of Neolithic quarrying for polished stone implement manufacture. Back on the road, drive S past a burnt mound at Skelberry (HU365869) to Housetter, where there are three chambered cairns, two beside the road, one high on the hillside (44). One of the cairns is reduced to a mound of rubble with two large uprights standing, so that it looks more like a pair of standing stones than a cairn.

S again on the A970, past the Brig of Collafirth (where there used to be a whaling station), there is a branch road to the radio stations on Collafirth Hill. Up this road, then W up the hill, is the simplest route to the top of Ronas Hill, Shetland's highest hill and the location of a chambered cairn (45) with a still-roofed chamber, although this may have been re-roofed since the Neolithic. In fine weather this is a superb walk with sweeping views, but in poor weather it is not worth doing for the cairn alone! A possible extension to this tour is to turn right at Swinister and drive along the S shore of Ronas Voe, with views of the red granite cliffs, to the old whaling station at Heylor (HU292810).

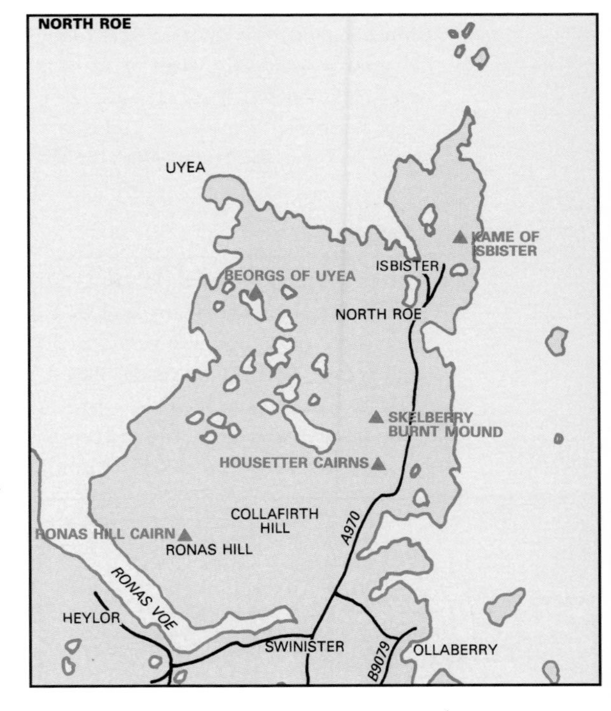

* Whalsay

Start from the ferry terminal at Symbister (HU537625). At the NE side of the bay are the remains of sixteenth/seventeenth-century Hanseatic Merchants' houses, one of which, the "Bremen Booth", has been restored (HU539625).

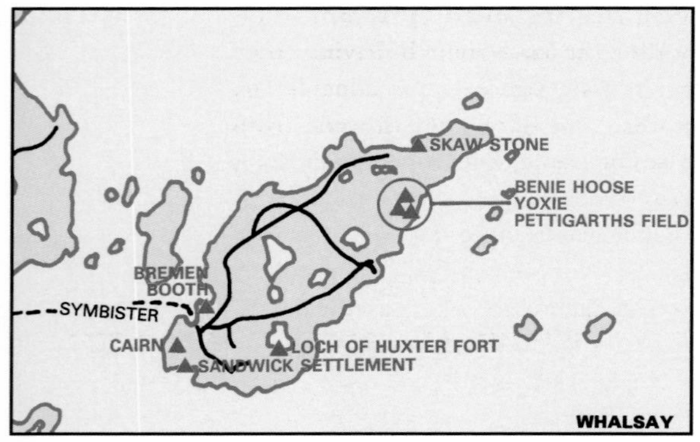

Continue along this road for 3km to the old quarry beside the road at Muckle Breck (HU586661). Park here and walk S to reach the excavated prehistoric houses at Yoxie, the Yoxie Stones (3) and the Benie Hoose (2), and the foundations of a miniature cairn on Pettigarths Field (40), overlooking them. Return to the road. There is a standing stone further NE at Skaw (39).

Backtrack to Brough and turn SW to Isbister and then to Loch of Huxter, with a fort on a little island (98). Continue on the road to the next left form, and turn down this to Sandwick. Walk down to the shore, where beside the loch are the remains of four prehistoric houses in a small field system, and also two burnt mounds (4). Return to the ferry terminal, and, if time permits, climb the small hill directly to the SW, which has a ruined chambered cairn on its summit (42).

* Fetlar

From the ferry terminal (HU582942), drive S for 1km, and then head W to Snabrough (95), not a broch but an eroding fort. Back on the road, follow it to Broch Lodge (HU581927), where a round tower stands on the site of a broch, and turn left onto the B9088. Branch right for Tresta, where beside a fine beach is the site of Papil, an early chapel location (HU604903). Beyond Tresta, as the road falls to the next bay, park and walk S to the site of the broch of Houbie (96), set just above the shore, and to its SW the traces of steatite working.

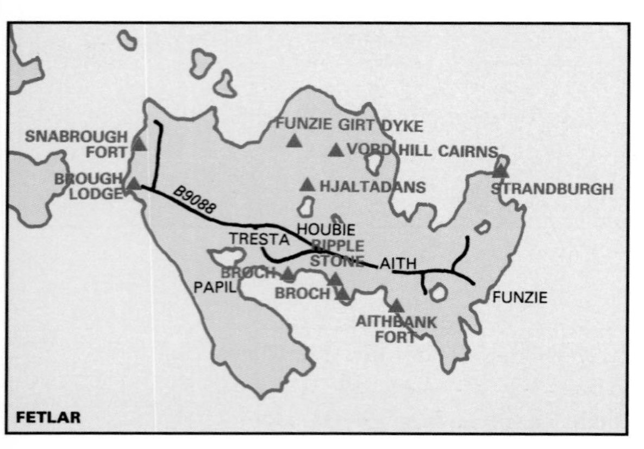

Rejoin the B9088 at Houbie, and continue SE, past the Ripple Stone (38) and the remains of the broch of Aith (HU629901). Beyond Wick of Aith, at Aithbank, there is a small multi-vallate fort on a headland (97). Follow the road to Funzie, from which the road N leads to Everland, from which it is a 2km walk to the monastic site at Strandburgh (125). Retracing the outward route, stay on the B9088 past the turn at Houbie, and, after 1km, turn up to the airstrip. Walk due N to Hjaltadans (37) and Vord Hill, which has two cairns on its summit (HU622936). The slope on the N and W side of Vord Hill is distinguished by the great boundary dyke of the Funzie Girt (1). (Note that this area falls within the RSPB Bird Reserve. Check locally before going past the airstrip.) Return to the road by the same route if driving. If on foot, it is possible, in reasonably dry summer weather, to proceed over moorland more or less direct to the ferry terminal.

South and Mid Yell

Arriving on the ferry at Ulsta (HU462795), the small island to the right, close in to Yell, is the Holm of Copister (HU472780), which has the remains of a broch with outer ramparts. On landing, proceed E along the B9081 Burravoe road past Kettlester burnt mound (68). At Burravoe the Old Haa has been converted into a visitor centre.

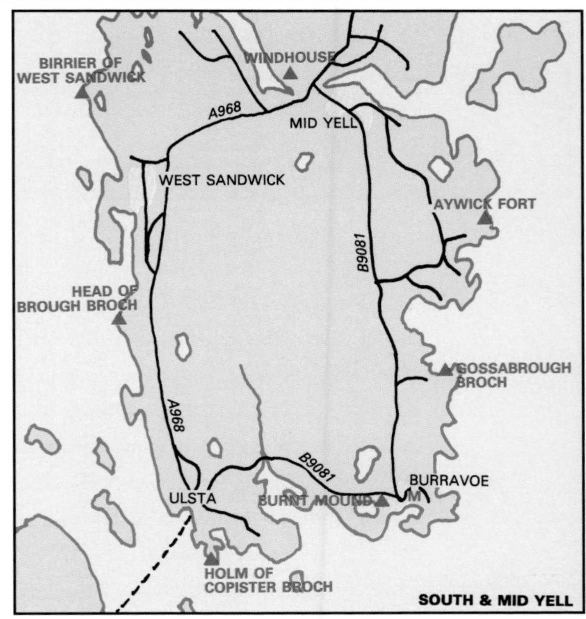

N on the B9081 Mid Yell road, after 3.5km a right-hand branch leads to Gossabrough (124). The broch here is flanked by slight traces of rectangular houses which may be of Norse date. Continue N, branching off next to Aywick, and take the more northerly of the two roads heading towards the E. 1km beyond the end of this, heading ENE, is the fort of Stoal (94), which was formerly believed to be a broch, but seems to be a simple multivallate promontory fort.

Proceed to Mid Yell (HU507908), and turn left onto the A968, back towards Ulsta. Not far along the road, on the right, at the head of Whale Firth, a ruined laird's house lies beside the more ruined foundations of a broch, while on the slope below it, not far above the water, is a small heel-shaped cairn (36), built against the slope and now represented by the facade alone. 3km further on, just as West Sandwick comes into view, there is a peat road to the right, and walking along this, past Ladie Loch and Mill Loch to Loch of Birriesgirt, the coast is reached, with a good view of the almost inaccessible monastic site at Birrier (117). Back on the main road, continue S, passing high above the Head of Brough (HU445849), where another ruined broch is located, and back to Ulsta.

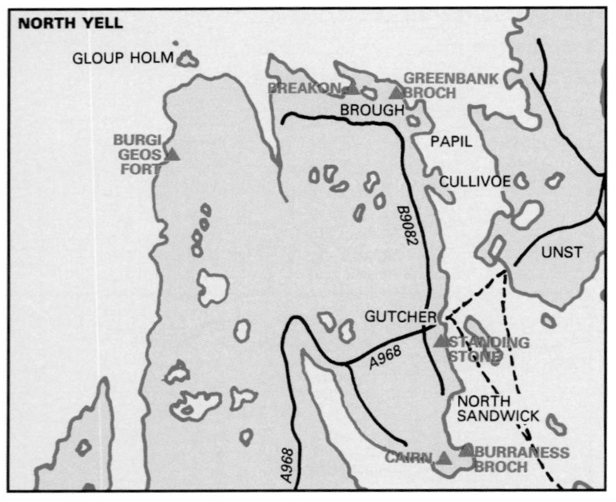

Start from the ferry terminal at Gutcher (HU548993). Take the main A968 road SW, and turn left to North Sandwick, passing a standing stone on the left (34). Park at the road end, and walk S to the bay and then, climbing above low cliffs, to Burra Ness (93). The broch is clearly visible to the E, and is flanked by reduced ramparts.

A number of boat nousts are to be seen on the shore W of the broch, and there are numbers of clearance cairns scattered about the peninsula, as well as a probable burial cairn 400m SW of the broch (HU553953). If visiting at early morning or dusk, this is one of the best places for chance spotting of an otter.

Returning to the car, drive N, joining the B9082, past Gutcher and Cullivoe to the North Yell school, where a branch road to the E leads to the chapel site at Papil (HP543041), although very little apart from the placename remains. 500m further along the main road, NE of Brough, a large green mound represents the broch of Greenbank (HP539051), and from this site for 1.5km to the W stretches the area of Breakon (33), or Breckon, which has a ruined church and burial ground and, among the sand dunes, a range of sites including prehistoric cairns, a house and field system, possible Pictish cairns and a Viking burial, the remains of Norse houses and, high up on the edge of the dunes, a seventeenth century fisherman's house, incorporating fragments of yellow Dutch brick, probably brought to Shetland as ballast.

Back on the B9082 road, follow this, and the unclassified extension, to the road end at Gloup (HP507046). The small island visible to the NW is Gloup Holm (HP486062), and many years ago traces of what may have been a broch were dug up on this very exposed location.

From Gloup a track leads S, past the memorial to the great fishing disaster at the end of the nineteenth century (ruined traces of a fishing station lie on the beach below), to the head of Gloup Voe, from which point head W up Rules Gill and over the moor to descend to the spectacular promontory fort at Burgi Geos (92). Return by the same route, and back to Gutcher.

Starting from the ferry terminal at Belmont (HP565005), leave the car and walk W round the bay to the broch of Hoga Ness (90), or Belmont, which has a fine set of ramparts. Back on the A968 road head NE, noting on the left the abandoned crofts and small lynchetted fields of the former settlement of Snarravoe (HP572023). Follow the B9084 to Uyeasound, and then, past the standing stones at Clivocast (32) to Muness Castle (HP629012), built at the very end of the sixteenth century. Returning towards Uyeasound, take a road to the N, to Hannigarth, and walk downhill to the S end of Sand Wick (123), where in a small area of sand dunes stand the remains of the thirteenth/fourteenth-century house and byre excavated in the early 1980s.

Return to Uyeasound and take the road past Gletna Kirk (HP592020) (which has a rather obscure history, but seems to have had some status as a healing site in Medieval times), onto the A968 then branching left to the Westing. (After 1km a track goes left past the massive standing stone at Bordastubble (31) and the old house of Lund to a ruined church and graveyard, beyond which is the monastic settlement on Blue Mull (116).) The road soon passes, on the left, the large mound of the broch of Underhoull (89) and its surrounding ramparts. Just downslope are the ruins of Norse houses excavated some years ago. These lay above Pictish and Iron Age houses (122). The road ends on the shore of a shingly bay, with a small island, Brough Holm, now eroding rapidly, which bears another broch (HP566058). Walk round the bay to the next headland N, where on a small knoll a recent building lies on the site of an early ecclesiastical establishment, probably a chapel and graveyard, called Kirkaby (HP566065). Return to the ferry at Belmont, or continue N towards Baltasound and the next tour.

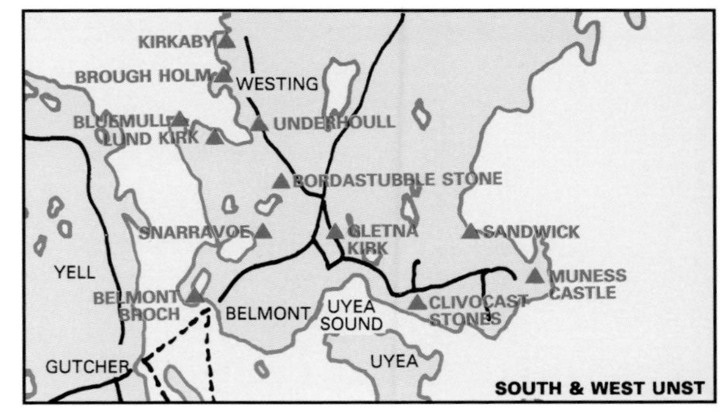

* North and East Unst

2km N of the Westing turn, the ruined cairn of Watlee (30) lies just to the W of the A968, and 2km further, the two cairns on Hill of Caldback (29) lie to the right. Descending towards Baltasound, go straight ahead, leaving the old chapel to the right. Park near the junction with an E-W road, and climb due N up Crussa Field, encountering just before the summit the three Rounds of Tivla (28). There are also two cairns on the summit. It is a pleasant walk, in good weather, to the E along the ridge of Nikka Vord to the cairns on Muckle Heog (27).

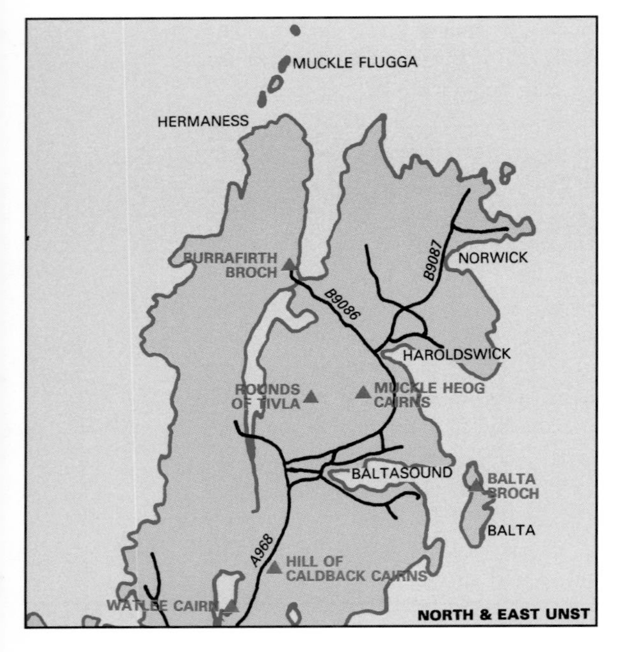

The striking rusty colouring of the rocks in this area reflects their unusual mineralogy: this area has been an important source of chromite and other chromium ores, and also of talc. The piers from which these minerals were shipped can be seen at Baltasound (HP633091). The end of the inlet is almost closed by a long island, Balta, on the seaward side of which stands a broch (HP660089).

Proceed N on the A968 to Haroldswick (HP636122), and then NW on the B9086 to Burrafirth, where a ruined broch stands beside Burra Firth (HP611143). From here a path runs N to Herma Ness (HP605183), from which can be seen the rock stacks of Muckle Flugga and Out Stack (HP612202), the most northerly point of the British Isles. Return to Haroldswick, and thus to Baltasound and the S.

Sites, monuments and landscapes

If you think you have found a new site, or wish further information locally about specific sites, contact:
Shetland Archaeologist,
22-24 North Road,
Lerwick,
ZE1 0NE.
(Telephone 0595 4688).

Telephone number changes

British Telecom expect to announce number changes to Shetland telephone numbers in 1994/95. If you experience difficulty dialling the telephone numbers detailed on pages 100, 110 or above ring the operator on 100 and ask for assistance.

Finds

If you think you have found an artefact, carved stone or other discovery, if possible leave it in place, but if not mark the spot clearly on the ground, so you can relocate it, and contact:
Shetland Museum,
Lower Hillhead,
Lerwick.
(Telephone 0595 5057).

Under Scots Law, all ancient objects must be reported for possible Treasure Trove action, not just objects of precious metal as in England.

FURTHER READING

Ashmore, P. J. *Jarlshof*, Edinburgh, 1993. (Historic Scotland guide.)

Berry, R. J. and Johnston, J. L. *The Natural History of Shetland*, London, 1980.

Crawford, B. E. *Scandinavian Scotland*, Leicester, 1987.

Crawford, B. E. (ed) *Essays in Shetland History*, Lerwick, 1984.

Fenton, A. and Palsson, H. (eds) *The Northern and Western Isles in the Viking World*, Edinburgh 1984.

Fojut, N. and Pringle, R. D. *The Ancient Monuments of Shetland*, Edinburgh, 1993. (Historic Scotland guide.)

Hamilton, J. R. C. *Excavations at Jarlshof, Shetland*, Edinburgh, 1956.

Hamilton, J. R. C. *Excavations at Clickhimin, Shetland*, Edinburgh, 1968.

Henshall, A. S. *The Chambered Tombs of Scotland, Vol. 1*, Edinburgh 1963.

Jakobsen, J. *An Etymological Dictionary of the Norn Language in Shetland*, Lerwick, 1985 (reprint).

Laing, L. *Orkney and Shetland. An Archaeological Guide*, Newton Abbot, 1974.

Morrison, I. *The North Sea Earls*, Edinburgh, 1973.

Nicolson, J. R. *Shetland*, Newton Abbot, 1972.

Ritchie, A. *Exploring Scotland's Heritage: Orkney and Shetland*, Edinburgh, 1985.

Ritchie, A. *Viking Scotland*, London, 1993.

Ritchie, G. and A. *Scotland: Archaeology and Early History*, London, 1981.

Royal Commission on the Ancient and Historic Monuments of Scotland *An Inventory of the Ancient and Historical Monuments of Orkney and Shetland*, Edinburgh, 1946.

Schei, L. K. and Moberg, G. *The Shetland Story*, London, 1988.

Smith, B. (ed) *Shetland Archaeology*, Lerwick, 1985.

Stewart, J. *Shetland Place-names*, Lerwick, 1987.

Turner, V. *How To Be A Detective*, Lerwick, 1991 (school textbook).

Maps

Ordnance Survey 1:50000 Landranger

Sheet 1 Shetland : Yell & Unst

2 Shetland : Whalsay

3 Shetland : North Mainland

4 Shetland : South Mainland

Partly rebuilt by "some gentlemen of Lerwick" in 1851, the broch of Clickimin nevertheless displays many classic features of broch architecture, such as this stair.

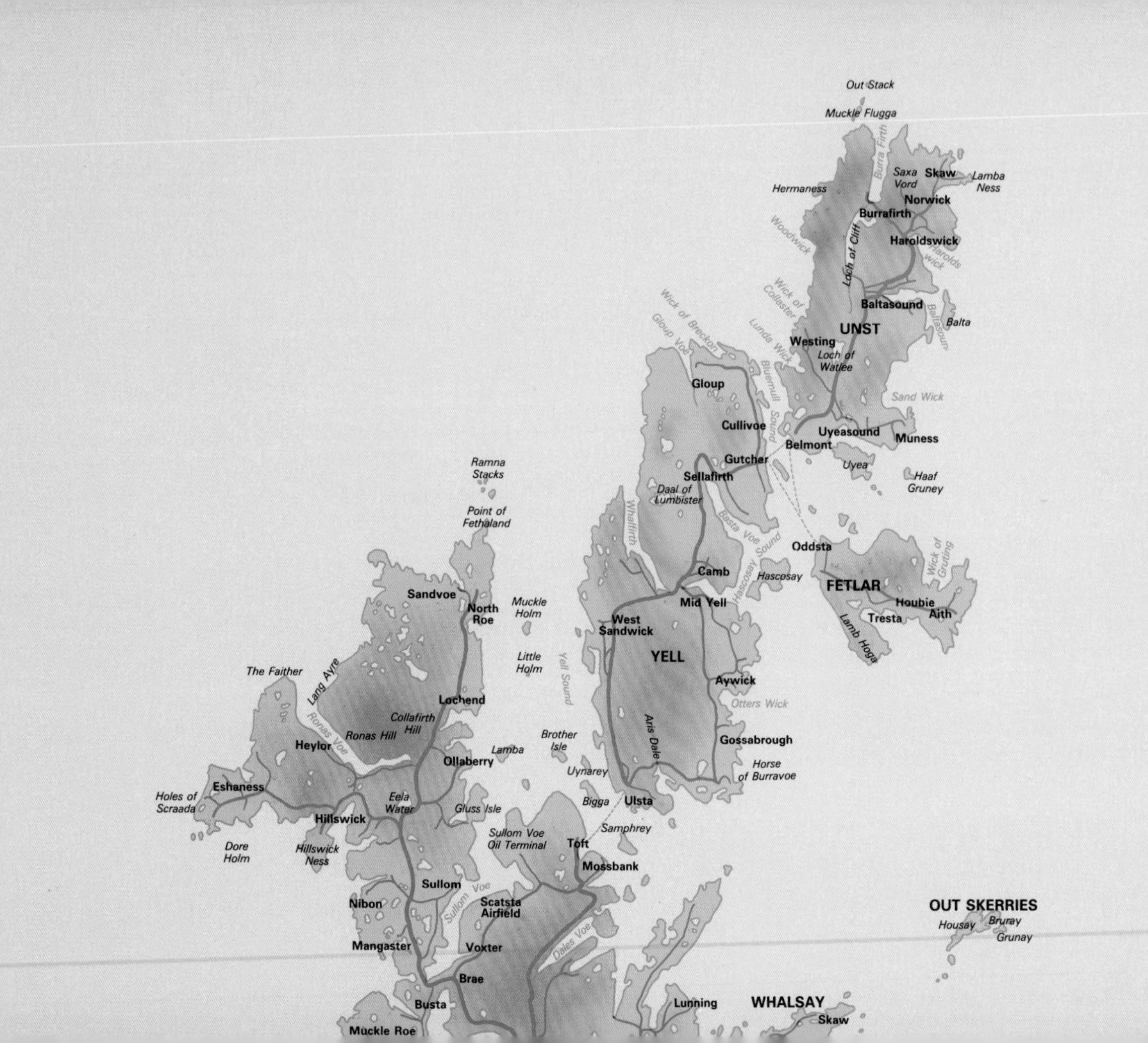

Out Stack
Muckle Flugga
Hermaness
Saxa Vord
Skaw
Lamba Ness
Norwick
Burrafirth
Burra Firth
Woodwick
Loch of Cliff
Haroldswick
Harolds wick
Wick of Collaster
Baltasound
Baltasoun
Balta
UNST
Westing
Loch of Watlee
Lunda Wick
Wick of Breckon
Gloup Voe
Gloup
Bluemull Sound
Sand Wick
Cullivoe
Uyeasound
Muness
Belmont
Uyea
Haaf Gruney
Gutcher
Sellafirth
Daal of Lumbister
Whalfirth
Basta Voe
Hascosay Sound
Oddsta
Wick of Gruting
Ramna Stacks
Point of Fethaland
Camb
Hascosay
FETLAR
Houbie
Aith
Tresta
Lamb Hoga
Sandvoe
North Roe
Muckle Holm
Mid Yell
West Sandwick
YELL
Little Holm
Yell Sound
The Faither
Lang Ayre
Lochend
Aywick
Otters Wick
Collafirth Hill
Ronas Hill
Ronas Voe
Heylor
Brother Isle
Lamba
Aris Dale
Gossabrough
Horse of Burravoe
Ollaberry
Uynarey
Eshaness
Holes of Scraada
Eela Water
Gluss Isle
Bigga
Ulsta
Hillswick
Samphrey
Dore Holm
Hillswick Ness
Sullom Voe Oil Terminal
Toft
Mossbank
Sullom
Sullom Voe
Nibon
Scatsta Airfield
OUT SKERRIES
Housay
Bruray
Grunay
Mangaster
Voxter
Dales Voe
Brae
Busta
Lunning
WHALSAY
Skaw
Muckle Roe